Guardians of the Gulf

A Deep Dive into the GCC Defence Industry

GEW Intelligence Unit

Global East-West (London)

Contents

Introduction

The defence industry in the Gulf Cooperation Council (GCC) states holds a significant place in the region's complex geopolitical landscape. Throughout the 20th century, the Arabian Peninsula witnessed many political and security challenges, which necessitated the development of robust military capabilities to protect national interests. The GCC states, including Bahrain, Kuwait, Oman, Qatar, Saudi Arabia, and the United Arab Emirates (UAE), sought to address these challenges by using defence procurement to strengthen their armed forces.

During the early stages of independence and state-building, the GCC states relied heavily on arms imports to equip and modernise their military establishments. The rationale behind this approach encompassed several factors. Firstly, the limited domestic industrial capabilities hindered the local production of complex defence systems. Secondly, the urgency to fortify their military capabilities in the face of evolving security threats necessitated access to advanced and reliable weaponry. Lastly, the GCC states aimed to establish regional deterrence by acquiring state-of-the-art defence systems, successfully deterring potential adversaries.

The United States emerged as a primary arms supplier to the GCC states in this period. With their vast military-industrial complex and longstanding strategic ties, the U.S. defence industry actively pursued opportunities to engage with the GCC states, fostering interdependence. These arms deals aided not only the defence industry itself but also contributed to strengthening U.S.-GCC alliances and supporting American interests in the region.

Nevertheless, as the GCC states gradually matured politically and economically, concerns surrounding supply chain vulnerabilities, overdependence on foreign powers, and rising costs emerged. These apprehensions prompted the GCC states to recognise the necessity of establishing their own indigenous defence industries, leading to a strategic shift from reliance on arms imports towards developing domestic capabilities.

Importance and Purpose of the Book

This book aims to comprehensively explore the strategic significance of the GCC states' defence industry, offering critical insights into its implications for regional security, economic development, and geopolitical dynamics. By examining the drivers and challenges surrounding the localisation of the defence industry in these states, it seeks to unravel the complex processes and factors that shape this evolving sector.

An in-depth analysis of the economic implications of indigenisation constitutes another significant aspect of this book. As the defence industry becomes increasingly localised, it holds the potential to generate substantial economic growth, create high-skilled job opportunities, and foster technological innovation. Scrutinising the economic dynamics and potential benefits of the defence industry in the GCC states offers valuable insights into their broader efforts towards economic diversification and reducing dependence on hydrocarbon revenues, ultimately facilitating the transition towards knowledge-based economies.

Aside from economic considerations, this book also explores the security implications of local defence industry development. As the GCC states endeavour to achieve defence indigenisation, there is potential for enhancing their military capabilities, reducing vulnerabilities, and strengthening their national security posture. Understanding the impact of these developments on regional security dynamics, military strategies, and collaborative defence initiatives is crucial for policymakers, security analysts, and defence officials.

Methodology and Structure

This book adopts a multidisciplinary approach to ensure a comprehensive and insightful analysis, integrating historical, economic, geopolitical, and security perspectives. The methodology encompasses primary research, including the analysis of arms import data, and detailed examination of secondary research, consisting of scholarly studies, reports, and expert opinions. This book aims to provide a holistic understanding of the GCC states' defence industry and its implications by triangulating various data sources and exploring diverse perspectives.

The book's structure follows a logical flow of information and analysis. Following this introductory chapter, which sets the stage by exploring the historical background, significance, and objectives of the GCC states' defence industry, subsequent chapters delve into the drivers and challenges of defence indigenisation, economic diversification, technology transfer, and innovation, as well as the impact on regional security cooperation. The book concludes by summarising the main findings and offering recommendations for policymakers and stakeholders.

In a region characterised by intricate political complexities and evolving strategic landscapes, this book offers valuable insights into the development of the GCC states' defence industry. By scrutinising the historical context, strategic significance, and multidimensional implications, this comprehensive resource caters to policymakers, defence officials, academics, and individuals interested in delving into the intricacies of the GCC states' defence industry and its far-reaching impact on regional and global dynamics.

Chapter 1

Significance and Objectives of the Book

The defence industry plays a pivotal role in the security and stability of nations, ensuring the protection of borders and critical infrastructure and safeguarding the interests of its citizens. Over the years, the Gulf Cooperation Council (GCC) states, comprised of Saudi Arabia, the United Arab Emirates, Bahrain, Kuwait, Oman, and Qatar, have heavily relied on arms imports from foreign suppliers to meet their defence requirements. However, there has been a growing realisation among these states about the importance of developing indigenous defence capabilities. As a result, the GCC states have increasingly focused on localising their defence industries.

Understanding the Motivations

Self-Reliance and Reducing Dependence

The pursuit of defence industry localisation in the GCC states is driven by a desire for self-reliance and reduced dependence on external suppliers.

Historically, the reliance on foreign imports has left them vulnerable to supply disruptions, geopolitical fluctuations, and potential limitations on advanced technologies. The GCC states aim to overcome these challenges and achieve greater self-sufficiency in meeting their defence needs by developing a robust defence industrial base. Localisation allows for nurturing domestic capabilities, enabling the GCC states to control and diversify their defence procurement sources.

Economic Diversification and Job Creation

The localisation of the defence industry also presents an opportunity for economic diversification and job creation in the GCC states. By developing local defence capabilities, these countries can enhance their industrial base, stimulate economic growth, and promote technological innovation. Establishing defence manufacturing facilities, research and development centres, and training institutions can create new job opportunities, reduce unemployment, and foster a skilled workforce.

Assessing the Implications

Economic Implications

Developing a local defence industry can benefit the GCC states significantly economically. It can boost the contribution of the defence sector to the overall GDP, attract foreign direct investment, and promote the export of defence products and services. Additionally, establishing defence industrial parks and clusters can stimulate the growth of related industries, such as advanced manufacturing, electronics, and IT sectors. This, in turn, can contribute to the overall economic diversification goals of the GCC states.

Security Implications

Localisation of the defence industry directly impacts the GCC states' security posture. These states can enhance their resilience and self-reliance by reducing dependence on external suppliers and fostering indigenous capabilities. With the ability to domestically produce and maintain defence equipment, the GCC states can mitigate risks associated with supply chain disruptions and more effectively respond to evolving threats. Localisation also enables the integration of advanced technologies, such as AI and cyber capabilities, into the defence sector, thereby enhancing overall defence capabilities and preparedness.

Geopolitical and Diplomatic Implications

The localisation process can reshape geopolitical dynamics in the Gulf region and beyond. The GCC states can potentially attain greater autonomy in their foreign relations and alliances by developing local defence industries. This strategic shift may lead to recalibrations of existing partnerships and the emergence of new collaborations. It can also influence the configuration of regional security dynamics and contribute to stability in the broader Middle East region. The localisation of defence industries also opens doors for collaboration and cooperation with global defence industry leaders, enabling technology transfer, joint ventures, and defence offset programmes.

Challenges and Considerations

The localisation of the defence industry in the GCC states is not without its challenges. Developing a competitive and sustainable local defence industry requires substantial investments in infrastructure, research and development, and human capital. The acquisition of advanced technologies and technical know-how from established defence industry players is another crucial aspect to consider. Overcoming these challenges necessitates strategic planning, policy coordination, and the establishment of robust legal and regulatory frameworks.

Scope and Structure of the Book

This book will be divided into several key sections to provide a comprehensive analysis of the localisation process in the GCC defence industry. The following chapters will explore the historical background and current trends, analyse the motivations and objectives of localisation, and assess the economic, security, and geopolitical implications. Specific attention will be given to case studies from countries such as Israel and Turkey to draw valuable lessons and identify best practices. Additionally, the book will delve into the challenges and opportunities in technology integration, diplomatic relations, and regional collaborations. By extensively examining these aspects, this book aims to contribute to a deeper understanding of the localisation process in the defence industry of the GCC states.

Through this chapter, the significance and objectives of the localisation of the defence industry in the GCC states have been thoroughly explored. Motivated by a desire for self-reliance, economic diversification, and enhanced security, the GCC states aim to reduce dependence on foreign suppliers and establish indigenous capabilities. The implications of this localisation process encompass economic growth, job creation, technological advancement, enhanced national security, geopolitical shifts, and the potential for diplomatic collaborations. Despite various challenges and considerations, the pursuit of localisation presents a significant opportunity for the GCC states to strengthen their defence capabilities and regional standing in a rapidly evolving global security landscape.

Methodology and Structure

The defence industry is vital in the Gulf Cooperation Council (GCC) states, which comprise Bahrain, Kuwait, Oman, Qatar, Saudi Arabia, and the United Arab Emirates (UAE). These countries have a long history of military cooperation and defence spending to ensure their national security and protect their economic interests. The importance of the defence industry in the GCC states cannot be underestimated, as it contributes significantly to their military capabilities, economic development, and geopolitical influence. This book is structured in a way that allows for systematically exploring the defence industry in the GCC states. Each chapter builds upon the previous one, providing a coherent narrative that progresses from historical developments to contemporary challenges and prospects.

Objectives of the Book

This book aims to comprehensively analyse the defence industry in the GCC states, exploring its historical development, current state, and future prospects. By examining the economic, security, and geopolitical implications of the localisation of the Gulf region's defence industry, this research sheds light on the strategic considerations, challenges, and opportunities the GCC states face.

The objectives of this book can be summarised as follows:

1. To analyse the historical evolution of the defence industry in the GCC states, taking into account the geopolitical and security dynamics that have shaped its trajectory.

2. To examine the drivers and strategies the GCC states employ to localise their defence industries, focusing on technological innovation, economic development, and national security.

3. To assess the economic implications of defence industry localisation, including job creation, technology transfer, and the potential for economic diversification.

4. To explore the security implications of localisation, particularly regarding military capabilities, deterrence, and regional stability.

5. To evaluate the geopolitical ramifications of defence industry localisation, including the influence on power dynamics within the region and beyond and the potential impact on global defence trade.

6. To analyse the diplomatic relations and collaborations resulting from the localisation of the defence industry, considering the redefinition of alliances and partnerships and the potential for greater regional cooperation.

7. To provide policy recommendations for the GCC states based on the research findings, identifying areas for further development and cooperation.

Chapter 2

Historical Background of the GCC States' Defense Industry

The strategic location of the GCC states has made them vulnerable to regional conflicts and security threats throughout history. These countries lie in a turbulent neighbourhood, surrounded by countries with varied political ideologies, ongoing conflicts, and simmering tensions. Over the years, the GCC states have faced various security challenges, including territorial disputes, regional rivalries, and external threats.

Throughout the 20th century, the GCC states' defence capabilities primarily relied on foreign military assistance and imports. During the colonial era, the Gulf states relied on the protection and influence of the British Empire. However, the withdrawal of British forces from the region in the 1970s and the subsequent Iranian revolution in 1979 marked a turning point in the security landscape of the GCC states. These events prompted the GCC states to invest heavily in their defence industries to achieve self-sufficiency and enhance their military capabilities to counter external threats.

The defence industry in the Gulf Cooperation Council (GCC) states has a rich and complex history that can be traced back to its colonial past and the subsequent geopolitical developments in the region. From the early 20th century until today, these countries have sought to establish and strengthen their defence capabilities to address security challenges and protect their national interests.

The GCC states, including Bahrain, Kuwait, Oman, Qatar, Saudi Arabia, and the United Arab Emirates (UAE), were historically under the influence of European colonial powers, such as Britain. This colonial legacy significantly shaped their defence strategies, as they inherited British military traditions and institutions during decolonisation.

During the early years of independence, the focus of the GCC states' defence policies was primarily on maintaining internal security and defending against external threats. The military forces were often small, more oriented towards internal security, and relied heavily on foreign assistance for equipment, training, and logistical support. British military advisers played a crucial role in training and modernising the armed forces of these countries.

However, the 1970s marked a turning point in the region's defence landscape. The GCC states experienced rapid economic growth due to the oil boom, leading to increasing political ambitions and security concerns. The rise of regional rivalries and conflicts, such as the Iran-Iraq War, the Gulf War, and regional power struggles, further underscored the need for stronger defence capabilities.

In response to these challenges, the GCC states began investing heavily in their defence sectors to modernise their armed forces and reduce their reliance on foreign assistance. They sought advanced weaponry and technology to enhance their military capabilities and establish a credible deterrence against potential threats. This shift in focus marked the beginning of a transformation in the region's defence industry.

The GCC states embarked on extensive arms procurement programmes to meet their growing defence requirements. They entered major deals with established defence industries in countries like the United States, the United Kingdom, France, and other European states. These deals facilitated the transfer of advanced military equipment, technology, and expertise to the GCC states – further contributing to the development of their defence industry.

Over time, the GCC states started to develop indigenous defence industries to meet their growing demand for advanced military equipment and technology. They established defence production facilities, research and development centres, and defence procurement agencies to enable self-sufficiency and reduce dependence on foreign suppliers. This localisation drive aimed to enhance military capabilities and stimulate economic diversification, job creation, and technological innovation.

In the 1990s and early 2000s, the GCC states continued their efforts to strengthen their defence industries. They focused on expanding their defence manufacturing capabilities, investing in research and development, and fostering partnerships with international defence companies and institutions. This resulted in significant advancements in aerospace, naval technology, land systems, and cyber defence.

Moreover, the GCC states also increased their domestic defence spending, allocating significant portions of their budgets to the defence sector to support the expansion and modernisation of their militaries. This financial commitment further contributed to the growth of their defence industries, supporting the development of critical infrastructure, capabilities, and human capital.

The historical background of the GCC states' defence industry is characterised by a trajectory of evolving security challenges, shifting alliances, and the pursuit of self-reliance. The defence sector has undergone significant growth and transformation from its colonial past to the present. Understanding this historical context is crucial for comprehending today's motivations and strategies behind the GCC states' defence industry.

The defence industries of the GCC states have demonstrated considerable progress and achieved notable milestones. For instance, Saudi Arabia established the King Abdulaziz City for Science and Technology (KACST) in 1985 to promote research and development in defence and strategic industries. KACST has played a pivotal role in enhancing the technological capabilities of Saudi Arabia's defence sector.

Similarly, the UAE has made significant strides in diversifying its defence industry by establishing companies like Emirates Defence Industries Company (EDIC), which focuses on defence manufacturing, maintenance, and repair across various sectors. EDIC's subsidiaries, such as Abu Dhabi Ship Building (ADSB), Emirates Advanced Investments Group (EAIG), and Tawazun Holding, have actively contributed to the expansion and localisation of the UAE's defence capabilities.

These endeavours have bolstered the GCC states' military strength and catalysed economic development. The defence industries have stimulated job creation, technology transfer, and the growth of local businesses through offset agreements and partnerships. They have also nurtured a skilled workforce, fostering specialised expertise and knowledge in defence-related fields.

Moreover, by developing their defence industries, the GCC states have reduced their reliance on foreign suppliers and enhanced their autonomy in decision-making. This shift has granted them greater control over their defence strategies, procurement processes, and production cycles. Additionally, it has reduced vulnerabilities associated with geopolitical shifts and fluctuations in global arms markets.

In recent years, the GCC states have further demonstrated their commitment to building robust defence industries by integrating emerging technologies into their military capabilities. They have invested in research and development centres to explore unmanned systems, artificial intelligence, cybersecurity, and space technology advancements.

The GCC states that the defence industry has not been without challenges, including technical, financial, and strategic hurdles. Ensuring a sustainable defence industrial base, fostering innovation, overcoming technology transfer barriers, and developing a skilled workforce remain key objectives for the GCC countries. Nonetheless, through continuous efforts and strategic investments, the GCC states have made significant progress in building indigenous defence industries that contribute to their national defence goals while bolstering their economic growth and technological capabilities.

In conclusion, the historical background of the GCC states' defence industry is marked by a transformation from relying on foreign assistance to establishing indigenous defence capabilities. The convergence of geopolitical dynamics, economic growth, and evolving security challenges has driven the GCC states to prioritise defence industry development. These efforts have led to manufacturing, research and development advancements, partnerships, and technological innovation. As the GCC states continue to invest in their defence industries, they aim to achieve a balanced mix of self-reliance, regional cooperation, and economic diversification to address both present and future security challenges.

Chapter 3

The Evolution of GCC States' Armed Forces

The Gulf Cooperation Council (GCC) states have a rich history of military organisations that dates back to ancient times. Historically, these regions were home to powerful empires built on conquest and defence. However, the establishment of modern armed forces in the GCC states took shape in the aftermath of World War II and during the post-colonial era.

In the 1950s and 1960s, the Gulf states faced various external threats and internal tensions, spurring the need for a more organised and equipped defence force. The emerging nations of Saudi Arabia, United Arab Emirates, Bahrain, Qatar, Kuwait, and Oman started to invest in building their armed forces, primarily with foreign aid and advisory support.

Challenges and Transformative Developments

The early phases of the GCC states' armed forces were marked by challenges such as limited resources, untrained manpower, and lack of infrastructure. The nascent nations heavily relied on foreign military personnel and advisors to establish and train their forces. However, they started investing in education and training programmes to nurture a local talent pool over time.

One of the significant challenges the GCC states faced was the constant rivalry between certain member states. Saudi Arabia and Iran, for example, have long had a tense relationship, which has complicated the regional security situation. This rivalry has often led to a race in military capabilities, with both countries seeking to outdo each other in terms of weaponry and defences.

Furthermore, the GCC states have had to contend with internal challenges, including tribal conflicts, political instability, and economic disparities. These issues have impacted the stability and cohesion within their armed forces. However, the GCC states have sought to address these problems through military reforms, promoting national unity and inclusivity within their armed forces.

Significant developments came in the 1970s and 1980s when the GCC states faced regional conflicts such as the Iran-Iraq War and the Gulf War. These conflicts accelerated the modernisation of armed forces with the inclusion of advanced weaponry, logistics, intelligence, and command and control systems. The GCC states also recognised the need for interoperability and joint operations to enhance collective defence capabilities.

Role of Modernisation in Shaping Military Capabilities

The GCC states have pursued ambitious modernisation programmes to strengthen their military capabilities in recent decades. To counter evolving security threats, they have sought to acquire advanced weapon systems, including combat aircraft, naval vessels, missile defence systems, and surveillance technology.

The modernisation drive has aimed to enhance the ability to project power regionally and protect vital national interests. The GCC states have also focused on enhancing their cybersecurity capabilities to confront the growing threats in the digital domain. Cybersecurity infrastructure development and training programmes have been implemented to protect critical infrastructure, government networks, and sensitive information.

Furthermore, the GCC states have prioritised force readiness, focusing on training and professionalism and increasing their operational capabilities. They have invested in modern training facilities, simulation technologies, and joint exercises with international partners to improve their effectiveness in combat. The GCC states have also introduced mandatory military service programmes, which help in national defence and contribute to national cohesion, as young individuals from diverse backgrounds serve together.

The evolution of the GCC states' armed forces has also necessitated improvements in defence partnerships and collaboration with international actors. Strategic alliances have shaped the GCC states' defence industry and military doctrines, particularly with the United States and other Western powers. These collaborations have resulted in technology transfers, joint military exercises, and the sharing of best practices, further enhancing the GCC states' military capabilities.

Moreover, the GCC states have recognised the importance of addressing non-traditional security challenges such as terrorism, cyber threats, and border security. This multidimensional approach has increased investment in intelligence gathering, surveillance systems, and cybersecurity infrastructure to safeguard national interests and protect critical infrastructure from potential attacks. Cooperation between the GCC states and international partners in intelligence sharing and counterterrorism efforts has been instrumental in combating extremist groups operating within the region.

In conclusion, the evolution of the GCC states' armed forces has seen a remarkable transformation from nascent organisations to modern and capable defence forces. The challenges faced by these nations have compelled them to invest in modernisation, establish strategic defence partnerships, and comprehensively address non-traditional security threats. Understanding these developments is crucial for comprehending the GCC defence industry's current dynamics and future prospects.

Chapter 4

Origins and Early Development

Origins and Early Development of the Armed Forces in the GCC

The origins of the armed forces in the Gulf Cooperation Council (GCC) states can be traced back to the tumultuous era of decolonisation and national self-determination that swept across the Arabian Peninsula during the mid-20th century. Following the dissolution of colonial empires and the departure of British and French forces from the region, the newly formed nations embarked on a journey to establish their own military institutions to defend their territorial integrity and maintain internal stability.

At their inception, the armed forces in the GCC states were relatively small and underdeveloped, reflecting the nascent nature of these countries. Comprising of modest infantry units and basic artillery, they sought to address immediate security concerns and address the challenges posed by regional dynamics. The general focus was on countering internal rebellions and external threats and maintaining law and order within their respective borders.

During this period, the GCC states relied heavily on the support of the British and other colonial powers who had previously controlled the region. British military advisors, in particular, played an instrumental role in training and developing the armed forces in the GCC states. This cooperation facilitated the transfer of military expertise, modern weaponry, and tactical knowledge, effectively helping these nations establish the foundations of their military institutions.

However, the geopolitical landscape of the Arabian Peninsula underwent significant changes in the 1970s and 1980s, leading to an increased need for modernised and expanded armed forces in the GCC. The Iran-Iraq War raging beyond their borders and the Soviet invasion of Afghanistan underscored the vulnerability of the Gulf region and the necessity of robust defence capabilities.

Recognising the evolving threats and challenges, the GCC states embarked on ambitious military modernisation programmes. Substantial financial investments were made to expand the size of their armed forces, acquire technologically advanced weaponry, and upgrade training and infrastructure.

The GCC states turned to foreign powers for support and collaboration to achieve these goals. The United States emerged as a primary partner, providing extensive military cooperation, arms sales, and military training programmes. Considered the cornerstone of the regional security architecture, this strategic alliance delivered substantial and sustained assistance to the GCC states' military development efforts.

The arms sales from the United States formed the backbone of the modernisation plans of the GCC states. They included procuring advanced fighter aircraft, missile defence systems, naval ships, and air defence capabilities. These acquisitions played a pivotal role in enhancing the GCC armed forces' operational capabilities and deterrence posture.

Beyond material acquisitions, the GCC states also sought to develop indigenous defence industries and increase domestic expertise in defence technologies. This involved establishing partnerships with foreign defence companies, promoting technology transfer and joint production ventures, and investing in research and development initiatives.

Alongside efforts to strengthen physical capabilities, the GCC states prioritised professionalisation and improving the training and education of their armed forces. Military academies were established, and foreign instructors were invited to share their expertise in various fields. This emphasis on professionalism aimed to develop effective leadership skills, foster a culture of discipline, and cultivate a sense of national identity and loyalty among the armed forces.

While the expansion and modernisation of the armed forces in the GCC faced challenges such as limited human resources, cultural sensitivities, and logistical constraints, the states demonstrated a remarkable commitment to overcoming these hurdles. By leveraging their substantial financial resources, strategic geographic location, and international partnerships, they managed to augment and diversify their defence capabilities successfully.

The early development of the armed forces in the GCC states laid the groundwork for their subsequent growth and modernisation. The focus on external threats, evolving regional dynamics, and the commitment to safeguard independence and stability led to the establishment of armed forces capable of defending the national interests of each GCC state.

In conclusion, the origins and early development of the armed forces in the GCC states were marked by the formation of independent military institutions, collaboration with foreign powers, and ambitious modernisation programmes. The integration of advanced weaponry, investment in training and education, and the cultivation of professional forces trans-formed the armed forces in the GCC states into capable and modern military establishments. This chapter has delved into the historical context, challenges, and transformative developments that shaped the early devel-opment of the armed forces in the Gulf region.

Chapter 5

Challenges and Transformative Developments

*T*his chapter explores the difficulties encountered by the military forces of the Gulf Cooperation Council (GCC) states and the significant changes that have impacted their development over the years. It is crucial to comprehend the historical background and the exceptional situations that have influenced the defence industry of this region.

The Gulf Cooperation Council (GCC) states, consisting of Bahrain, Kuwait, Oman, Qatar, Saudi Arabia, and the United Arab Emirates, established their armed forces primarily in response to regional security threats and the need to safeguard their sovereignty. Many of these countries had limited military infrastructure before their independence, relying on ad hoc local forces or colonial structures for security.

During the early years, these nascent armed forces faced significant challenges in building their capabilities. They relied heavily on foreign assistance and expertise to overcome these hurdles. Western nations, particularly the United States and the United Kingdom, played a crucial role in providing training, equipment, and military advice to help establish and shape the defence institutions of the GCC states. This external support had a lasting impact on their military doctrines and operational strategies.

Challenges and Transformative Developments

Geopolitical Rivalries and Regional Conflicts:

The armed forces of the GCC states have confronted numerous challenges arising from geopolitical rivalries and regional conflicts. One of the most prominent rivalries has been with Iran, a regional power with its own regional ambitions. Various factors, including territorial disputes, ideological differences, and the struggle for influence have driven the tensions between GCC states and Iran.

The Iran-Iraq war (1980-1988) had a profound impact on the security paradigm of the region. It highlighted the vulnerability of the GCC states and their need for robust defence capabilities. The armed forces were forced to reassess their defence strategies and enhance their military readiness to counter threats from neighbouring countries.

The Gulf War (1990-1991), sparked by Iraq's invasion of Kuwait, had a transformative impact on the armed forces of the GCC states. It led to the introduction of multinational forces, particularly under the umbrella of the United Nations, highlighting the importance of international cooperation in addressing regional crises. This conflict showcased the need for stronger defence partnerships and the significance of strategic alliances in ensuring regional stability.

The ongoing conflicts in Yemen and Syria continue to pose significant challenges for regional security. These conflicts have intensified sectarian tensions, provided a breeding ground for extremism, and strained the resources and capabilities of the armed forces. The GCC states have had to deploy forces and contribute to multinational efforts to address these conflicts, exposing them to the complexities of modern warfare and asymmetric threats.

Security Threats and Counterterrorism:

The GCC states face security threats arising from a range of sources, including terrorism, extremism, insurgency, and internal unrest. Organisations such as Al-Qaeda and the Islamic State have exploited socioeconomic grievances, religious divides, and political instability to advance their ideologies and perpetrate acts of violence.

In response, the armed forces of the GCC states have established specialised counterterrorism units and invested in intelligence capabilities. They have recognised the importance of proactive measures such as pre-emptive strikes, intelligence-driven operations, and targeted assassinations against high-value targets to disrupt terror networks. International partnerships, particularly with the United States, have played a vital role in providing intelligence sharing, training, and technical support to counter these threats.

Furthermore, the GCC states have focused on combating the financing of terrorism and strengthening their borders and critical infrastructure against infiltration. Investments in advanced surveillance systems, biometric technologies, and intelligence-sharing platforms have contributed to deterring and identifying potential security threats.

Technological Advancements and Modernisation Efforts:

Technological advancements have played a transformative role in shaping the armed forces of the GCC states. The rapid development of advanced weaponry, precision-guided systems, and unmanned aerial vehicles (UAVs) has significantly impacted their defence capabilities and operational effectiveness.

The GCC states have devoted considerable resources to modernising their armed forces to keep pace with these advancements. They have pursued comprehensive defence acquisition programmes, procuring sophisticated military hardware such as fighter jets, missile defence systems, naval vessels, and command and control systems. These modernisation efforts aim to enhance deterrence capabilities, establish a credible defence posture, and reduce dependency on foreign military assistance.

At the same time, the GCC states have also recognised the importance of investing in indigenous defence industries to foster self-sufficiency and reduce reliance on foreign sources. They aim to nurture local expertise, create job opportunities, and strengthen their defence industrial base by developing research and development capabilities and promoting defence technology sectors.

Defence Cooperation and Alliances:

The armed forces of the GCC states have sought to strengthen their defence capacities through various forms of cooperation and alliances. They have cultivated robust partnerships with countries such as the United States, the United Kingdom, France, and others, enabling the transfer of technology, knowledge exchange, and joint military exercises.

The United States has been a key strategic partner for the GCC states, offering training programmes, technical assistance, and defence equipment. The signing of bilateral defence agreements and establishing military bases have further solidified these partnerships. These alliances provide the GCC states with military support and contribute to their diplomatic clout and regional influence.

In recent years, defence cooperation within the GCC has gained prominence. The establishment of the Peninsula Shield Force, a joint military intervention force, reflects the collective efforts of the member states to enhance their collective defence capabilities. Furthermore, the GCC states have engaged in joint naval patrols, intelligence sharing, and border security cooperation to address the common challenges of maritime security and counterterrorism. These initiatives foster greater coordination, interoperability, and mutual understanding among the armed forces of the GCC.

Evolution of Military Doctrines and Strategies

The evolving security landscape and technological advancements have necessitated the adaptation of military doctrines and operational strategies. The armed forces of the GCC states have transitioned from traditional conventional warfare concepts to incorporating asymmetric warfare capabilities, including cyber warfare, special operations forces, and electronic warfare.

Asymmetric warfare capabilities have become increasingly significant in countering non-state actors and adapting to the nature of conflicts in the region. Cyber warfare presents new challenges, requiring the development of robust cybersecurity measures and the ability to conduct offensive and defensive cyber operations. Special operations forces have played a critical role in counterterrorism operations, intelligence gathering, and unconventional warfare.

Furthermore, the concept of jointness has gained prominence in the armed forces of the GCC states. It emphasises the integration of various military branches and the coordination of joint operations. Joint training exercises and the development of combined task forces have become paramount to ensure seamless coordination, interoperability, and strategic mobility across different branches of the armed forces.

Looking Toward the Future:

The challenges and transformative developments discussed in this chapter provide a foundation for understanding the trajectory of the armed forces of the GCC states. The future holds further challenges and opportunities as the region faces the uncertainties of the evolving global and regional security landscapes.

The armed forces must anticipate and adapt to emerging threats such as cyber warfare, hybrid warfare, and the proliferation of ballistic missiles. Investments in research and development, defence industry localisation, and human capital development will become vital to maintain the technological edge, reduce dependency on foreign sources, and ensure long-term security sustainability.

While external security concerns remain of utmost importance, the armed forces must strike a balance with internal stability. Addressing socioeconomic disparities, promoting inclusivity, and leveraging soft power tools will be critical in countering extremist ideologies, addressing grievances, and maintaining social cohesion.

Collaboration and cooperation among the armed forces of the GCC states will be crucial in ensuring collective security and addressing regional challenges. Building upon the existing framework of defence cooperation, there is a need further to enhance interoperability, information sharing, and joint exercises. This will strengthen their collective defence capabilities, deter potential aggressors, and contribute to regional stability.

International partnerships and alliances will continue to play a pivotal role in the future of the armed forces of the GCC states. Strengthening relationships with countries such as the United States, the United Kingdom, and France will provide access to advanced military technologies, training opportunities, and intelligence sharing. Additionally, exploring partnerships with emerging powers such as China, India, and Russia can diversify defence cooperation and open up new avenues of collaboration.

The GCC states must also focus on diversifying their economies and reducing their dependence on oil revenue. Economic diversification will strengthen their overall resilience and enhance their defence capabilities by providing a sustainable funding source for the armed forces. Investing in research and development, technology transfer, and defence industries will create jobs, build local expertise, and foster innovation.

The evolving role of the armed forces in the GCC states will extend beyond traditional defence and security concerns. They will be called upon to participate in humanitarian assistance and disaster relief efforts, peacekeeping missions, and regional initiatives. This expanded role reflects the growing expectations for these armed forces to contribute to global stability and security.

In conclusion, the armed forces of the GCC states have faced and continue to face numerous challenges. Geopolitical rivalries, security threats, technological advancements, and the need for defence cooperation have shaped their evolution over time. Looking toward the future, these armed forces must adapt to emerging challenges, strengthen partnerships, invest in technological advancements, and contribute to regional and global security. The armed forces of the GCC states have a critical role to play in preserving the region's stability, security, and prosperity.

Chapter 6

Role of Modernisation in Shaping Military Capabilities

Throughout history, the modernisation of armed forces has played a crucial role in determining their capabilities and effectiveness. The GCC states have recognised the significance of modernisation in meeting the evolving challenges of regional security and have actively pursued efforts to enhance their military capabilities.

The process of modernisation involves the adoption of advanced technologies, equipment, and tactics to enhance the effectiveness of military forces. Modernised armed forces can deter potential threats, swiftly respond to crises, and protect national interests. With their strategic location and unique security concerns, the GCC states have placed considerable emphasis on modernising their armed forces.

One of the key drivers of modernisation in the GCC states is the need to counter emerging threats and maintain a credible deterrent posture. The region has witnessed significant geopolitical shifts and the proliferation of advanced military technologies, including those related to cyber warfare, unmanned systems, and long-range precision-guided munitions. These factors have necessitated the adoption of modernised defence systems to ensure the security and stability of the GCC states.

The GCC states have pursued a multi-faceted approach to fulfil these modernisation goals. Firstly, they have actively sought to acquire advanced weaponry and equipment from international suppliers. For example, Saudi Arabia has demonstrated its commitment to modernisation by conducting major military acquisitions, such as procuring advanced fighter aircraft, naval vessels, and missile defence systems. Similarly, the United Arab Emirates has invested in advanced missile defence systems, fighter jets, and surveillance aircraft.

However, modernisation efforts in the GCC states go beyond acquiring advanced weaponry and equipment. It also involves the development of indigenous defence industries, the establishment of robust research and development capabilities, and the fostering of a skilled workforce. By investing in these areas, the GCC states aim to reduce their dependence on foreign suppliers and enhance their self-reliance in meeting defence needs. Developing domestic defence industries also fosters economic diversification, job creation, and technology transfer.

The growth of indigenous defence industries has been a key aspect of the modernisation drive in the GCC states. For example, Saudi Arabia has taken significant strides in establishing a domestic defence industry by partnering with international companies to set up joint ventures and technology transfer agreements. The country has also created research and development centres to foster innovation and enhance indigenous capabilities. This approach not only enhances the military capabilities of the GCC states but also has positive economic effects by creating job opportunities, attracting foreign investment, and developing a skilled workforce.

Furthermore, modernisation enables the GCC states to strengthen their interoperability and compatibility with international partners, particularly the United States and other Western allies. By aligning their defence systems and procedures with those of their counterparts, the GCC states enhance their ability to participate in joint military operations and benefit from collective defence arrangements. The transfer of technology, expertise, and best practices that come with modernisation collaborations significantly strengthens the capabilities of the GCC armed forces.

Beyond military considerations, modernisation initiatives in the GCC states also play a pivotal role in social and economic development. The defence sector represents a significant source of job creation and technological innovation. By investing in domestic defence industries, the GCC states enhance their security, stimulate economic diversification, and reduce reliance on hydrocarbon revenues. The growth of a robust defence industry contributes to long-term stability and sustainability by promoting the development of human capital and advanced technological know-how.

In the face of modern security challenges, the GCC states also place great importance on non-conventional capabilities. With the rising prominence of cyber threats, intelligence, surveillance, and reconnaissance (ISR) systems have become instrumental in determining military effectiveness. The ability to gather real-time intelligence, analyse data, and respond in a timely manner has become essential. Modernisation efforts encompass developing and integrating advanced command and control systems, information-sharing platforms, and cyber defence mechanisms. The GCC states strengthen their resilience against hybrid threats and asymmetric warfare techniques by doing so.

Moreover, modernisation efforts in the GCC states extend beyond hardware and technology. They also focus on the enhancement of training and doctrine. Comprehensive modernisation involves updating military doctrines to adapt to emerging challenges, maximising equipment utilisation, and ensuring efficient operational planning. By investing in training and skills development, the armed forces of the GCC states become more proficient in utilising modern technologies. They can effectively respond to a vast array of security threats.

In conclusion, modernisation plays a pivotal role in shaping the military capabilities of the GCC states. Adopting advanced technologies, developing domestic defence industries, and enhancing non-conventional capabilities allow the GCC states to counter emerging threats and enhance regional security effectively. Moreover, modernisation efforts foster interoperability with international partners, stimulate economic growth, and promote long-term stability. The ongoing commitment to modernisation in the GCC states ensures their national security and the maintenance of regional stability in an ever-changing security landscape.

Chapter 7

Arms Imports and Defense Dynamics in the GCC

With rapid economic growth and increasing security challenges, the Gulf Cooperation Council (GCC) states have heavily relied on arms imports to meet their defence needs. This chapter aims to analyse the arms import data from the Stockholm International Peace Research Institute (SIPRI) and explore the implications of these imports on the defence dynamics in the GCC.

The GCC states have consistently ranked among the world's largest importers of defence equipment, and their arms imports have risen significantly over the past decades. The data provided by the SIPRI Arms Transfers Database reveals the extent and patterns of arms imports in the region and offers valuable insights into the defence cooperation between the GCC states and their primary suppliers.

The United States has been a major arms supplier to the GCC states, accounting for a significant portion of their imports. This close defence relationship between the United States and the GCC countries can be attributed to several factors. Firstly, shared security interests and concerns about regional stability have fostered a mutual interest in defence cooperation. Secondly, the GCC states' desire to enhance their military capabilities and modernise their armed forces has driven them to turn to the United States, which offers advanced weaponry and state-of-the-art defence systems.

A closer examination of the arms import data reveals interesting trends and dynamics within the GCC. Saudi Arabia is by far the largest arms importer in the region, with a significant proportion of its imports comprising major combat systems such as combat aircraft, vehicles, ships, and missiles. The country's strategic location, role as a key regional player, and ongoing military engagements have necessitated a sizable defence procurement strategy.

The United Arab Emirates (UAE) follows Saudi Arabia regarding arms imports. Like its neighbour, it has significantly invested in advanced defence systems such as fighter aircraft, armoured vehicles, and missile defence. The UAE's aim to develop a robust and technologically advanced military and its proactive approach to defence cooperation has led to a considerable inflow of arms from various suppliers.

Qatar, another prominent GCC state, has made substantial progress in its defence capabilities and has become a significant arms importer. The country's ambitious defence modernisation plans, including expanding its air force and procuring naval vessels, have resulted in an increased demand for defence equipment. Furthermore, Qatar's hosting of major international sporting events and its growing regional influence have contributed to its efforts to enhance its defence capabilities.

Kuwait, Bahrain, and Oman also feature in the arms import data, albeit to a lesser extent than Saudi Arabia, the UAE, and Qatar. These countries have gradually modernised their armed forces, acquiring equipment such as armoured vehicles, patrol boats, and air defence systems. While their defence imports may be comparatively lower, they still play an important role in maintaining regional stability and addressing security concerns.

The heavy reliance on arms imports raises questions of vulnerability and dependency for the GCC states. While the inflow of advanced weaponry has enhanced their capabilities, it also poses challenges in terms of sustainability and self-reliance. Recognising this, the GCC states have increasingly focused on developing indigenous defence industries and promoting technology transfer through offset arrangements.

In recent years, a growing emphasis has been on localising the defence industry in the GCC states. Efforts to diversify and develop domestic defence capabilities have gained momentum, aiming to reduce reliance on imports and foster self-sufficiency. These efforts include establishing defence industrial zones, joint ventures with international defence companies, and investments in research and development.

For instance, Saudi Arabia's Vision 2030 plan includes the goal of localising 50% of the country's military spending by 2030, fostering the growth of the defence industry and encouraging technology transfer and knowledge exchange. The plan sets the stage for a comprehensive overhaul of the defence sector, encompassing defence procurement and domestic defence production, export capabilities, and skilled workforce development.

Similarly, the UAE's defence strategy strongly emphasises fostering domestic defence industry capabilities through partnerships with international defence companies and investments in research and development. The country aims to develop a sustainable, competitive, and globally recognised defence industry that can contribute to the nation's defence needs and become an exporter of defence products.

Qatar's efforts are also significant, with the establishment of the Qatar Armed Forces Industry Committee (AFIC) and the Qatar Defence Manufacturing Committee (DMC) focusing on enhancing local defence production capabilities and reducing reliance on imports. The country actively seeks partnerships and joint ventures with international defence companies to develop indigenous manufacturing capabilities and promote technology transfer.

The progress made by the GCC states in promoting self-reliance and reducing their dependency on arms imports is evident. However, achieving full self-sufficiency in defence production remains a long-term goal, necessitating continuous investments in research and development, technology acquisition, and skilled manpower.

Furthermore, the chapter explores the implications of arms imports on regional security dynamics. The heavy inflow of advanced weaponry has led to a regional arms race, where each GCC state seeks to enhance its military capabilities and maintain a balance of power. This arms race can potentially destabilise the region, as the accumulation of arms and defensive technologies may fuel tensions among states, heightening the risk of conflicts.

However, the GCC states have also recognised the importance of regional security cooperation to mitigate the risks associated with the arms race. Efforts such as joint military exercises, coordinated defence strategies, and defence capability sharing have been pursued to enhance collective security and maintain regional stability. Initiatives like the Peninsula Shield Force, a joint military defence initiative, aim to promote unity and interoperability among the GCC states' armed forces, allowing for a coordinated response to regional security challenges.

In conclusion, this extended chapter comprehensively analyses the arms imports and defence dynamics in the GCC states. It highlights the significance of arms imports in enhancing the military capabilities of the GCC states while also shedding light on the challenges of vulnerability and dependency. The chapter underscores the efforts made by the GCC states to localise their defence industries and reduce reliance on imports. It also delves into the implications of arms imports on regional security dynamics, emphasising the importance of maintaining a delicate balance to avoid escalating arms races or conflicts. Such insights are crucial for policymakers and officials to make informed decisions regarding defence procurement strategies and regional security cooperation.

Chapter 8

Analysis of Arms Import Data from SIPRI

*I*n this chapter, we will explore the arms import data provided by SIPRI *(Stockholm International Peace Research Institute) to gain a better understanding of the dynamics and patterns of arms acquisition in the Gulf Cooperation Council (GCC) states. SIPRI has been monitoring and analyzing arms transfers between countries since the 1950s, which provides a solid foundation for comprehending the global arms trade.*

By carefully examining the arms import data, we aim to understand the trends, drivers, and implications of defence procurements in the GCC region. Our analysis encompasses the overall volume of imports and the specific types of weapons systems and technologies acquired over the years. This in-depth examination offers key indicators of the GCC states' military capabilities and strategic objectives.

The data from SIPRI reveals that the GCC states have consistently increased their arms imports over time, underscoring their commitment to maintaining robust defence capabilities. Between 2011 and 2020, the GCC states accounted for approximately 10% of global arms imports, placing them among the most active regions in terms of defence procurements. During this period, Saudi Arabia emerged as the leading arms importer in the region, responsible for 35% of the total GCC imports. The United Arab Emirates (UAE) and Qatar were closely behind, accounting for 17% and 14% of total GCC imports.

The data from the Stockholm International Peace Research Institute (SIPRI) does indicate that some Gulf Cooperation Council (GCC) states are among the world's largest importers of arms. According to the SIPRI fact sheets, Saudi Arabia and Qatar are listed among the top five arms importers globally for the period 2018–22. This suggests that at least some GCC states have indeed been increasing their arms imports over time.

However, the search results do not provide a specific time-series analysis of arms imports by all GCC states, nor do they confirm a consistent increase across all GCC members. The results from SIPRI highlight that the Middle East, which includes the GCC states, accounted for 31% of global arms imports in 2018–22, and that there was an overall decrease in arms transfers to the Middle East by 8.8% between the periods 2013–17 and 2018–22. This indicates that while individual GCC states like Saudi Arabia and Qatar are significant arms importers, the region as a whole has seen a slight decrease in arms imports.

It is important to note that the SIPRI data is based on the transfers of major arms and does not necessarily reflect the total defence spending or the entirety of military procurement, which can include other forms of military equipment and services. Additionally, the data from SIPRI is often the best available open-source information, but it may not capture all arms transfers due to the secretive nature of some defence deals.

A closer examination of the major arms suppliers to the GCC states reveals a dynamic landscape with shifting dynamics. Historically, the United States and European countries, including the United Kingdom, France, and Germany, have been the primary sources of arms for the GCC states. However, there has been an observable diversification of suppliers in recent years. Russia and China have increasingly become major players in the arms trade with the GCC states, offering advanced systems and technologies. This diversification highlights the GCC states' pursuit of varied sources to enhance their defence capabilities and reduce dependence on any single supplier.

Nevertheless, while specific GCC states such as Saudi Arabia and Qatar are among the top arms importers in the world, the search results do not conclusively show that all GCC states have consistently increased their arms imports over time. Instead, there has been a slight regional decrease in the Middle East's arms imports according to the period comparisons provided by SIPRI.

To gain deeper insights into the military strategies and priorities of the GCC states, it is essential to look at the specific types of weapons systems they have acquired. Between 2016 and 2020, aircraft constituted the largest share of imports, accounting for 48% of total GCC arms imports. This focus on air power reflects the GCC states' endeavours to bolster their capabilities in aerial warfare and defence. Armoured vehicles followed closely behind with a 19% share, emphasising the significance of ground strength. Naval vessels accounted for 13% of imports, highlighting the GCC states' recognition of the importance of securing their waters and coastal regions. Missiles constituted 8% of imports, emphasising missile defence capabilities. The remaining 12% comprised other military equipment necessary for a comprehensive defence arsenal.

While the arms imports exemplify the commitment of the GCC states to developing robust defence capabilities, they also raise concerns about potential arms races and the risk of conflict escalation. The increased military capabilities among the GCC states have created a delicate balance of power in the region, with potential implications for stability and peace. It is vital to approach this issue cautiously and promote transparent dialogue and confidence-building measures to ensure regional security and stability.

Furthermore, the arms import data from SIPRI sheds light on the defence cooperation between the GCC states and the United States. The United States, as a longstanding ally and strategic partner in the region, has been a prominent supplier of advanced weaponry to the GCC states. This partnership not only bolsters the defence capabilities of the GCC states but also aligns their security interests with those of the United States. It underscores the geopolitical significance of the GCC region and the strategic importance of maintaining stable relationships with nations within the region.

However, the extensive reliance on arms imports also raises questions about the level of dependence on external suppliers and the potential implications for national security and autonomy. The GCC states have recognised the need to reduce their import reliance and develop indigenous defence capabilities. Consequently, efforts to localise the defence industry and promote defence manufacturing within the GCC states have gained momentum in recent years. These initiatives aim to enhance self-sufficiency in defence production, reduce vulnerabilities associated with external supply chains, and foster technological innovation within the region.

By understanding the arms import data from SIPRI, we can draw valuable conclusions about the defence dynamics in the GCC region. This analysis provides crucial insights into the GCC states' military capabilities, strategies, and vulnerabilities. Moreover, it serves as a foundation for the subsequent chapters, where we will explore the progress made by the GCC states in developing domestic defence industries, reducing reliance on arms imports, and fostering self-reliance in defence procurement.

Chapter 9

Insights into Defense Cooperation with the United States

*D*efence cooperation between the Gulf Cooperation Council (GCC) states and the United States has been a significant aspect of the region's security dynamics for decades. This chapter aims to comprehensively understand the nature and intricacies of defence cooperation between the GCC states and the United States and its broader implications.

Historical Context of Defence Cooperation:

The roots of defence cooperation between the GCC states and the United States can be traced back to the early 20th century. As the United States emerged as a global power, its interest in the stability of the Gulf region increased. The GCC states sought closer ties with the United States to strengthen their defence industries and capabilities, recognising the need for enhanced security capabilities. This marked the beginning of a longstanding partnership that has evolved over time.

Procurement of Advanced Military Equipment and Technologies:

A central aspect of defence cooperation has been procuring advanced military equipment and technologies from the United States. The GCC states have sought cutting-edge weaponry and platforms to bolster their defence capabilities and ensure regional stability. Over the years, the United States has been a leading supplier, providing the GCC states with state-of-the-art fighter jets, armoured vehicles, air defence systems, naval vessels, and intelligence-gathering equipment. This collaboration has allowed the GCC states to maintain a deterrent posture and develop a formidable military presence.

The procurement process involves negotiations, agreements, and technical evaluations. The United States, one of the world's largest defence producers, offers various options for the GCC states to choose from, ensuring their specific defence needs are met. These equipment and technologies undergo rigorous testing and certification to ensure the highest performance and reliability standards. Furthermore, the procurement contracts often involve the purchase of equipment and the transfer of technology and knowledge, allowing the GCC states to enhance their indigenous defence industries and build self-sufficiency.

Defence Training and Education Programmes:

Complementing the acquisition of advanced military equipment, defence training, and education programmes have played a crucial role in strengthening the defence cooperation between the GCC states and the United States. The GCC states have sent their military personnel to the United States for training, where they have had access to world-class facilities and expertise. These programmes have focused on various areas, including tactical training, leadership development, joint operations, and specialised courses on emerging defence technologies.

The training programmes offered by the United States are tailored to meet the specific needs of the GCC states. This includes preparing military personnel for asymmetric warfare and counter-terrorism operations and addressing the evolving security challenges in the region. The training exchanges also facilitate the sharing of best practices, lessons learnt, and cultural understanding between the armed forces of the GCC states and the United States. Moreover, the joint exercises conducted during the training programmes enhance interoperability, allowing the forces from both sides to operate seamlessly during joint ventures, such as multinational exercises or contingency responses.

Advisory and Technical Assistance:

Beyond equipment procurement and training, the United States has provided advisory and technical assistance to the GCC states. This collaboration has aimed to strengthen their defence capabilities and institutionalise necessary reforms in their armed forces. The United States has worked closely with the GCC states through regular consultations and dialogue to identify their specific defence requirements, assess their existing capabilities, and develop strategies to address gaps.

Areas of advisory and technical assistance have included command and control systems, intelligence sharing, cyber defence, counter-terrorism strategies, logistics, and maintenance practices. The expertise and guidance offered by the United States have allowed the GCC states to develop robust defence institutions, enhance their operational capabilities, and improve overall defence governance. The assistance also includes capacity building to foster regional cooperation in sharing intelligence, coordinating responses to common threats, and establishing effective crisis management mechanisms.

Strategic Implications:

The defence cooperation between the GCC states and the United States has had broad strategic implications for both sides. The United States has provided a security umbrella for the GCC states, deterring potential threats and ensuring regional stability. This alignment has fostered trust and confidence in the region, allowing the GCC states to focus on economic development, social progress, and other aspects of nation-building. Moreover, the defence cooperation has contributed to regional deterrence against regional or transnational adversaries, reinforcing the collective security of the GCC states.

From the perspective of the United States, defence cooperation with the GCC states has facilitated access to strategic military bases, logistical support, and intelligence-sharing hubs in the Gulf region. This enables the United States to project its power, maintain a presence in a vital geopolitical area, and safeguard its national interests. Moreover, the GCC states' enhanced defence capabilities contribute to burden-sharing in regional security, allowing the United States to allocate its resources to other areas worldwide.

Challenges and Limitations:

Despite the overall success of defence cooperation, challenges and limitations have also emerged. Chief among these are the regional rivalries and political dynamics that occasionally impact the nature and extent of defence cooperation between the GCC states and the United States. The

GCC states' diverse security perspectives and interests sometimes lead to divergence in priorities, limiting the extent to which a unified defence strategy can be formulated and implemented.

Conflicting interests and security concerns within the Gulf region have sometimes complicated collaborative efforts. Political disputes, such as those related to regional conflicts or diplomatic tensions, can strain defence cooperation and hinder joint initiatives. Additionally, disparities in defence capabilities and technological gaps between the United States and the GCC states can pose challenges in fully leveraging defence cooperation. The need to overcome interoperability issues and build local capacity in defence industries remains a constant focus for both sides.

In conclusion, defence cooperation with the United States has been a vital component of the security policies and capabilities of the GCC states. Through arms procurement, training programmes, advisory assistance, and strategic alignment, the GCC states have significantly enhanced their defence capabilities and benefited from the United States' security support. This deeper understanding of defence cooperation sheds light on the dynamics of the defence industry in the Gulf region and its wider implications for regional security and stability. It remains essential for the GCC states and the United States to continue nurturing this partnership, adapt to evolving challenges, and explore new avenues to strengthen defence cooperation in an ever-changing security landscape.

Chapter 10

Implications of Arms Imports on Regional Security

A *rms imports play a significant role in shaping the regional security dynamics of the Gulf Cooperation Council (GCC) states. This chapter explores the implications of arms imports on regional security and analyses the various factors.*

The historical context of arms imports in the GCC states can be traced back to the early 20th century when these countries lacked a strong indigenous defence industry and relied on foreign military equipment and technologies to build their defence capabilities. This dependency was largely driven by security challenges in the region, including regional conflicts, territorial disputes, and the perceived threat from Iran.

Arms imports from various countries, particularly the United States, have been extensive in the GCC states. These imports have both positive and negative implications for regional security. On one hand, they contribute to the capabilities of the GCC states and act as a deterrent against potential adversaries. Western-made advanced weapon systems, such as fighter aircraft, missile defence systems, and naval vessels, enhance the defensive capabilities of the region.

The United States has been the primary supplier of arms to the GCC states, driven by the strategic partnership and shared interests in maintaining regional stability. Over the years, this close relationship has resulted in substantial transfers of advanced military equipment. Not only does this benefit the GCC states in terms of enhancing their military capabilities, but it also serves as a means for the United States to exert influence and maintain a presence in the region.

However, arms imports also introduce certain vulnerabilities and challenges. One of the major concerns is the risk of technological dependence on foreign suppliers. While the GCC states acquire advanced military hardware, they rely on the suppliers for spare parts, maintenance, and upgrades. Any disruption in the supply chain due to political or economic factors can compromise the region's security. The issue of technological dependence can also restrict the GCC states' ability to decide autonomously on defence matters, potentially compromising their strategic interests.

Moreover, the flow of arms into the region can fuel arms races and increase tensions between neighbouring countries. The GCC states' arms build-up can be misinterpreted by regional rivals as an aggressive stance, leading to a potential escalation of conflicts. This arms race dynamic can further destabilise the region and hinder prospects for cooperation and peaceful resolutions.

The imbalance in military capabilities resulting from arms imports can also lead to a regional power shift and the potential for conflict. For instance, acquiring advanced fighter aircraft by one GCC state may generate concerns among its neighbours, prompting them to seek their own advanced weaponry to maintain a balance of power. This pattern can create an environment of instability and insecurity, where regional rivalries are reinforced and trust erodes.

Another implication of arms imports on regional security is the influence of foreign powers. Arms suppliers often attach conditions and restrictions to the use of these weapons, potentially constraining the GCC states' autonomy in defence decision-making. Regional security dynamics are then intertwined with the geopolitical interests of external players. For example, the United States has occasionally leveraged its position as a key arms supplier to influence the GCC states' foreign policies or actions, particularly to Iran.

The presence of foreign military advisors and technicians accompanying arms transfers further deepens the influence of external powers in the region. While their purpose is often to assist with training, maintenance, and interoperability, their involvement can create challenges in balancing national security interests with external influences. It is crucial for the GCC states to navigate these dynamics carefully to avoid compromising their sovereignty and decision-making autonomy.

The GCC states have initiated efforts to develop their own defence industries to mitigate the potential negative implications of arms imports. The localisation of the defence industry aims to reduce dependency on foreign suppliers and enhance self-reliance in meeting the countries' defence needs. This drive towards indigenisation can help minimise vulnerabilities and provide greater control over defence matters, indirectly strengthening regional security.

The localisation of the defence industry also brings about economic benefits, such as job creation, technology transfer, and the development of a skilled workforce. The GCC states can foster innovation and diversify their economies beyond oil dependence by investing in domestic defence capabilities. This contributes to enhancing regional security and improves the long-term sustainability of the countries.

The GCC states have also been exploring opportunities for regional defence cooperation and integration to strengthen their collective security further. Initiatives like the Gulf Defence and Security Cooperation Agreement, known as the "Riyadh Pact," aim to enhance joint military capabilities, information sharing, and coordination among the member states. This approach allows for pooling resources and expertise, reducing duplications and maximising regional security.

However, challenges remain in achieving proper regional defence integration. Differences in national interests, varying threat perceptions, and historical rivalries can hinder progress. Additionally, the influence of external powers in the region can complicate efforts to build a cohesive regional security framework. Nevertheless, the GCC recognises the importance of building a resilient security architecture to address common threats and challenges.

In conclusion, arms imports significantly affect regional security in the GCC states. While they contribute to enhancing the defensive capabilities of the region, they also introduce vulnerabilities, potential arms races, and geopolitical influences. The historical context, strategic partnerships, and external forces shape the dynamics of arms imports in the region. The efforts to localise the defence industry, promote regional defence cooperation, and strengthen collective security are important steps towards minimising these implications and promoting greater regional security. By reducing dependency on foreign suppliers, fostering self-reliance, and enhancing regional cooperation, the GCC states can navigate the complexities of arms imports and protect their strategic interests in an evolving security landscape.

Chapter 11

The Drive for Localisation of the Defence Industry

Strategic and Autonomy Considerations

The localisation of the defence industry has become a key strategic goal for the Gulf Cooperation Council (GCC) states. This drive is motivated by a desire to achieve greater autonomy in their defence capabilities and reduce reliance on foreign suppliers. By developing a robust indigenous defence industry, these states aim to enhance their national security and ensure the sustainability of their military capabilities. Strategic considerations play a vital role in this endeavour, allowing the GCC states to have more control over the defence technologies and resources they require.

Minimising External Dependencies

One of the primary objectives of localising the defence industry is to minimise external dependencies and enhance national security. The GCC states have historically relied heavily on arms imports from other countries, which can leave them vulnerable to disruptions in supply chains or changes in political dynamics. By fostering the growth of their defence industry, these states can reduce their reliance on external sources, ensuring the continuous availability of critical defence equipment and technologies.

Moreover, reducing external dependencies also helps safeguard national security interests. By decreasing reliance on foreign suppliers, the GCC states can mitigate the risk of potential embargoes or limitations on arms sales that could be imposed during times of political tension or conflict. Being self-sufficient in defence production allows these states to maintain their military readiness regardless of external circumstances, safeguarding their sovereignty and strategic interests.

Technology Transfer and Self-Reliance

Localisation of the defence industry also facilitates technology transfer and fosters self-reliance. In the process of developing their indigenous defence capabilities, the GCC states seek to acquire advanced technologies and know-how from established defence industries. This technology transfer enhances their military capabilities and promotes knowledge and technological advancements in other sectors of the economy.

The benefits of technology transfer extend beyond defence needs. The expertise gained through collaboration with international defence contractors can be utilised in other industries, leading to the development of high-tech sectors such as aerospace, manufacturing, and information technology. The GCC states can build a knowledge-based economy that transcends military applications by nurturing indigenous defence industries.

Moreover, self-reliance in defence production can have a positive economic impact. It creates jobs and stimulates technological innovation, contributing to the overall growth and diversification of the economy. The defence industry catalyzes research and development, leading to advancements in various scientific fields with wider applications beyond the defence sector.

The GCC states are actively investing in research and development, establishing defence research centres, and forging collaborations with international defence contractors to achieve these goals. By aligning their defence industry localisation efforts with national economic development plans, the GCC states aim to leverage the defence sector as a driver of economic growth and diversification.

Furthermore, by localising the defence industry, the GCC states can exercise greater control over the customisation of defence equipment according to their specific needs. This customisation capability is crucial in promoting interoperability among different regional defence systems. The GCC states often engage in joint military operations and exercises, and having the flexibility to customise defence equipment enhances their ability to work seamlessly together.

In addition, the localisation of the defence industry strengthens the domestic defence supply chain. Rather than relying on foreign suppliers for spare parts or maintenance services, the GCC states can develop a robust local ecosystem of suppliers and service providers. This not only ensures the availability of critical resources but also boosts the capabilities of domestic industries, leading to job creation and economic growth.

The localisation of the defence industry also contributes to the development of a skilled workforce. As the GCC states invest in building indigenous defence capabilities, they focus on training and educating their citizens in defence-related fields. This creates employment opportunities and reduces the need for foreign experts, fostering the development of a highly skilled workforce that can contribute to other sectors of the economy.

Furthermore, localising the defence industry allows for greater control over intellectual property rights. Developing their own defence technologies and systems allows the GCC states to protect their innovations and prevent unauthorised access to critical defence capabilities. This ensures the confidentiality and security of sensitive information and technologies, safeguarding their strategic interests.

In conclusion, the drive for localisation of the defence industry in the GCC states is driven by strategic considerations, the need for autonomy, and the desire to minimise external dependencies while promoting national security and economic growth. Through technology transfer, self-reliance, customisation capabilities, and the strengthening of domestic supply chains, the GCC states aim to enhance their military capabilities, improve interoperability among regional defence systems, create jobs, and foster innovation. The localisation of the defence industry is a multi-faceted endeavour that encompasses not only defence-related goals but also broader socio-economic objectives. It is a testament to the GCC states' commitment to national security and aspirations for strategic autonomy in an increasingly complex geopolitical landscape.

Chapter 12

Strategic and Autonomy Considerations

*I*n this chapter, we will be discussing the strategic and autonomous factors *that lead to the localization of the defence industry in the Gulf Cooperation Council (GCC) states. These factors are of utmost importance as the GCC nations aim to reduce their reliance on external sources, strengthen their self-sufficiency, and boost their national security capabilities.*

The strategic imperative to reduce vulnerabilities is one of the primary motivations behind the drive for localisation in the defence sector. The GCC states have recognised the risks associated with relying heavily on foreign defence suppliers, especially in times of geopolitical tensions or potential disruptions in the international arms market. Substantial reliance on external sources for military equipment and technology limits the GCC countries' autonomy and leaves them vulnerable to supply chain disruptions and political influence by external actors. By localising their defence industries, these countries aim to reduce these vulnerabilities and ensure continuous access to critical military equipment and technologies.

Furthermore, achieving autonomy in the defence sector aligns with the broader strategic goals of the GCC states. It allows them greater control over their military capabilities, decision-making processes, and national security strategies. By reducing their reliance on foreign defence suppliers, the GCC countries improve their ability to respond swiftly and effectively to emerging threats and changing geopolitical dynamics. This autonomy provides the GCC countries with the freedom to shape their defence postures by their unique geopolitical circumstances, regional dynamics, and national security interests.

Reducing reliance on external defence suppliers also facilitates technology transfer and the development of indigenous capabilities. The localisation of the defence industry allows for the domestic production of advanced weaponry and systems, thereby enhancing the technological prowess of the GCC states. This, in turn, strengthens their overall defence capabilities and paves the way for significant advancements in military technology. Developing indigenous defence capabilities reduces reliance on foreign suppliers and stimulates innovation, research, and development within the GCC states. The advancement of technology within the region fosters knowledge transfer, enhances the intellectual capital of the Gulf states, and positions them as global leaders in defence technology and innovation.

Moreover, localisation brings economic and industrial benefits to the GCC states. By building their own defence industries, these countries create new job opportunities, stimulate technological innovation, and attract foreign investment. The defence sector acts as a catalyst for economic growth, generating revenue and contributing to the diversification of the GCC economies. It promotes the development of a skilled workforce, fostering the growth of specialised industries related to defence, such as manufacturing, engineering, and research and development. The spillover effects of the defence industry further contribute to the growth of other sectors, creating a multiplier effect that strengthens the overall national economy.

Additionally, localisation in the defence industry nurtures strategic partnerships and collaborations with other nations. The GCC states actively seek collaboration with established defence industries worldwide to learn from their experiences, gain access to cutting-edge technologies, and build interdependencies that further enhance their autonomy and strategic independence. Through joint ventures, technology transfer agreements, and research partnerships, the GCC states leverage the expertise of foreign defence industries while concurrently boosting their own knowledge base and capabilities.

While strategic considerations drive the push for localisation, it has challenges. Developing a robust defence industry requires substantial financial investments, technological know-how, and skilled human resources. The GCC states must carefully balance these considerations to ensure their defence industries' effective and sustainable development. Government support in terms of financial allocations, policies, regulations, and incentives is crucial to creating an enabling environment for the growth of the defence sector. Simultaneously, investing in education and vocational training programmes that focus on defence-related fields helps cultivate a skilled workforce capable of meeting the sector's demands.

Furthermore, effective technology transfer necessitates the establishment of research and development centres, advanced manufacturing facilities, and testing and evaluation centres within the GCC countries. This infrastructure accelerates the development and production of indigenous defence technologies and contributes to overall technological advancement and innovation in the region. Collaboration and knowledge sharing with established defence industries are critical to fostering skills transfer and technology absorption.

In conclusion, strategic and autonomy considerations play a critical role in driving the localisation of the defence industry in the GCC states. By reducing external dependencies, increasing autonomy, and fostering indigenous capabilities and technological advancements, the GCC countries aim to strengthen their national security, stimulate economic growth, and position themselves as self-reliant in defence matters. Recognising and addressing these strategic imperatives is key to understanding the motivations behind the localisation efforts in the defence sector in the Gulf region. Through careful planning, investments in research and development, and collaboration with global defence industries, the GCC states can successfully build and sustain robust domestic defence industries that bolster their strategic autonomy and resilience.

Chapter 13

Minimising External Dependencies

The Gulf Cooperation Council (GCC) states have taken significant measures to strengthen their defence capabilities and achieve greater strategic autonomy. They aim to reduce their external dependencies in the defence industry. This chapter provides a comprehensive analysis of the various strategies employed by these states to minimize their reliance on foreign sources for military equipment and technology. It also examines the implementation and outcomes of each strategy.

The Gulf Cooperation Council's Growing Concerns:

The GCC states face numerous challenges and vulnerabilities when heavily relying on foreign defence suppliers. These concerns include potential political and economic entanglements, risks of embargoes or supply disruptions, the need for tailored defence solutions, and the desire for local job creation and economic growth. Therefore, to safeguard their national security interests and ensure the continuity of military capabilities even during times of geopolitical uncertainties, the GCC states have embarked on a multi-faceted approach to minimise external dependencies.

Technology Transfer and Indigenous Innovation:

An essential aspect of minimising external dependencies is technology transfer. The GCC states have actively sought partnerships and collaborations with defence manufacturers willing to transfer critical technologies and expertise. Leveraging their significant buying power and market potential, these states strive to negotiate favourable transfer agreements allowing state-of-the-art technologies to be acquired. Such transfers are facilitated through licencing agreements, joint ventures, direct investment in research and development (R&D), or the purchase of proprietary production capabilities. The GCC states aim to build their indigenous defence industries by procuring or developing cutting-edge technologies, reducing reliance on foreign suppliers and customising solutions to meet their unique requirements. Additionally, fostering indigenous innovation through targeted R&D initiatives enables the development of next-generation defence capabilities, keeping the GCC states at the forefront of technology.

Emphasising Defence R&D:

The GCC states have made significant investments in defence research and development, recognising the need for technological innovation and indigenous development. They have established dedicated defence R&D centres and collaborated with local universities and research institutions to create an ecosystem that fosters innovation and knowledge creation. Besides addressing immediate defence requirements, these endeavours contribute to the region's overall scientific and technological progress. Through these partnerships, the GCC states are encouraging knowledge transfer from academia to industry, supporting the development of homegrown talent, and facilitating the commercialisation of defence research outcomes. Furthermore, these investments lay the foundation for a sustainable defence industry by nurturing a skilled workforce and creating a culture of innovation and technological advancement.

Industrial Partnerships and Joint Ventures:

To accelerate the development of their defence industries, the GCC states have actively sought strategic industrial partnerships and joint ventures with foreign defence companies. These partnerships encompass various areas such as manufacturing, technology transfer, training and skills development, and knowledge sharing. By collaborating with established defence manufacturers, the GCC states gain access to advanced production techniques, specialised skills, and global supply chains, enhancing their ability to manufacture world-class defence equipment. These partnerships also provide an avenue for knowledge and technology transfer, enabling the GCC states to develop local manufacturing capabilities and foster the growth of a domestic defence industrial base. In addition to the economic benefits, such industrial partnerships enhance the self-sufficiency and long-term sustainability of the GCC states' defence sectors.

Localisation of Defence Production:

Localising defence production and supply chains is crucial for minimising external dependencies. The GCC states have adopted policies encouraging domestic production of defence equipment and components. By establishing local manufacturing capabilities, they reduce vulnerability to supply chain disruptions, embargoes, or export restrictions imposed by foreign suppliers. Localisation efforts encompass the entire defence supply chain, including design, development, production, assembly, integration, and maintenance. To incentivise local production, the GCC states provide fiscal incentives and R&D grants and promote joint ventures between foreign defence companies and local partners. Additionally, these efforts contribute to economic growth by creating job opportunities, fostering the growth of local industries, and developing associated sectors such as logistics, maintenance, and repair.

Knowledge and Skills Development:

The GCC states recognise the importance of developing a skilled workforce to support their defence industries. They have invested significantly in education and vocational training programmes to create a pipeline of skilled professionals, engineers, and technicians. Through collaborations with local and international educational institutions, the GCC states ensure their defence workforce possesses the necessary technical skills, knowledge, and expertise. These programmes cover a wide range of disciplines, including engineering, science, technology, and management. They are designed to cultivate a homegrown talent pool capable of maintaining, operating, and innovating upon locally produced defence equipment. Moreover, continuous professional development initiatives and exchange programmes with foreign defence organisations contribute to the growth and expertise of the defence workforce.

Strategic Stockpiling and Redundancy:

The GCC states have paid attention to strategic stockpiling and redundancy to mitigate the risks associated with supply chain vulnerabilities and disruptions. These states maintain adequate reserves of critical defence components, spare parts, and ammunition as part of their strategic planning. This stockpiling ensures the operational readiness of their military forces, even during emergencies or supply shortages. Moreover, creating redundancies in defence supply chains allows for greater flexibility and alternative sourcing options. By diversifying suppliers, establishing strategic partnerships with multiple countries, and acquiring or developing dual-use technologies, the GCC states enhance their resilience to geopolitical upheavals and disruptions in global markets.

Conclusion:

The GCC states are actively reducing their external dependencies in the defence sector through a comprehensive set of strategies. By leveraging technology transfer, emphasising defence R&D, fostering strategic industrial partnerships, localising defence production and supply chains, developing knowledge and skills, and implementing strategic stockpiling and redundancy measures, these states are working toward achieving strategic autonomy and self-reliance in defence capabilities. Pursuing these objectives not only enhances their national security interests but also stimulates economic growth, fosters technological advancements, promotes job creation, and strengthens regional stability. The long-term success of these strategies relies on sustained investment, continuous adaptation to evolving security challenges, and effective collaboration with domestic and international stakeholders.

Chapter 14

Technology Transfer and Self-Reliance

I n the constantly changing global defence industry, technology transfer has become an essential element for nations aspiring to improve their military capabilities and achieve self-sufficiency. This chapter provides a detailed understanding of the importance of technology transfer and its impact on self-sufficiency in the defence industry context within the GCC states.

1. Understanding Technology Transfer:

1.1 Definition and Types of Technology Transfer:

Technology transfer refers to sharing or transferring knowledge, expertise, and advanced technology from one entity to another. This can occur through various means, such as licencing agreements, joint ventures, collaborative research, or reverse engineering.

1.2 Importance for Defence Industry Modernisation:

Technology transfer plays a pivotal role in modernising defence industries by facilitating the acquisition of advanced military technologies, fostering indigenous capabilities, reducing reliance on foreign sources, and enhancing national security and self-sufficiency.

1.3 Key Players in Technology Transfer Processes:

Technology transfer involves multiple actors, including government agencies, defence contractors, research institutions, and educational organisations. Collaboration among these stakeholders is crucial for effective knowledge exchange and successful technology transfer.

2. Historical Perspective:

2.1 The GCC States' Dependence on Foreign Technology:

Historically, the GCC states have heavily relied on foreign nations to meet their defence technology needs due to limited local capabilities or lack of indigenous technological development.

2.2 Challenges Faced in Acquiring Advanced Technologies:

The acquisition of cutting-edge defence technologies can present numerous challenges, including high costs, complex regulations, limited access to proprietary information, and the need for skilled technicians and engineers capable of utilising acquired technologies.

2.3 Efforts towards Technology Transfer and Localisation:

The GCC states have made significant efforts to pursue technology trans-fer and localisation initiatives, recognising the need to decrease dependence on foreign sources. These endeavours include establishing joint ventures, integrating offsets, fostering domestic research and development (R&D), and developing specialised educational programmes.

3. Strategic Implications:

3.1 Reducing Dependency on Foreign Sources:

Technology transfer allows the GCC states to decrease their reliance on foreign defence suppliers. By acquiring critical technologies locally, they can enhance their strategic autonomy, reduce vulnerabilities associated with international dependencies, and maintain operational readiness dur-ing geopolitical volatility.

3.2 Enhancing Autonomy and National Security:

Establishing a robust technology transfer framework enables the GCC states to maintain control over their defence systems' critical components, maintenance, and upgrades. This enhances their self-reliance, sovereignty, and national security.

3.3 Fostering Indigenous Technological Capabilities:

By pursuing technology transfer, the GCC states can foster the growth of indigenous defence industries. This, in turn, stimulates local economic development, promotes job creation, encourages innovation and knowledge-sharing, and bolsters the development of a skilled workforce and intellectual capital.

4. Technology Transfer Models:

4.1 Bilateral Agreements and Collaborations:

Bilateral agreements and collaborations between the GCC states and technologically advanced nations serve as a key conduit for technology transfer. These agreements typically involve exchanging knowledge, skills, and technologies through joint research programmes, training, and know-how transfer.

4.2 Offsets and Industrial Cooperation Programmes:

Offsets and industrial cooperation programmes stipulate that foreign defence suppliers invest in local industries, transfer technology, or engage in joint ventures to compensate for defence purchases. These initiatives promote technology transfer by encouraging foreign firms to share advanced know-how with local entities.

4.3 Role of Innovation and Research Institutions:

Innovation and research institutions play a critical role in facilitating technology transfer. By engaging in collaborative research projects and fostering technological innovation, these institutions contribute to developing indigenous defence capabilities and encourage knowledge diffusion.

5. Successful Cases:

5.1 Examples of Technology Transfer in the GCC Defence Industry:

The GCC states have witnessed notable success in technology transfer initiatives. Examples include establishing local defence manufacturing capabilities, joint development of military vehicles, indigenous production of unmanned systems, and the localisation of maintenance, repair, and overhaul (MRO) capabilities.

5.2 Lessons Learnt and Best Practices:

Examining successful cases reveals valuable lessons for effective technology transfer. These include establishing strong partnerships, investing in research and development, creating supportive policy frameworks, fostering a culture of innovation, and promoting collaborations between academia, industry, and the government.

5.3 Achieving Technological Self-Reliance:

Successful technology transfer initiatives enable the GCC states to enhance their technological self-reliance. By combining acquired technologies with local capabilities, they can develop sustainable defence industries capable of meeting their own operational requirements and potentially exporting defence products.

6. Challenges and Constraints:

6.1 Technological Gaps and Technological Catch-Up:

Bridging technological gaps and catching up with technologically advanced nations pose significant challenges. Rapid advancements in defence
technologies and stringent export control regimes can potentially limit the
effectiveness of technology transfer initiatives.

6.2 Intellectual Property Rights and Licencing Issues:

Intellectual property rights (IPR) and licencing considerations are vital
in technology transfer agreements. Establishing appropriate IPR frameworks, licencing provisions, and legal safeguards is essential to protect the
interests of both technology providers and recipients.

6.3 Ensuring Compatibility and Interoperability:

Achieving seamless integration and interoperability between the acquired
technologies and existing defence systems can be challenging. Standardisa-
tion efforts, effective testing procedures, and the establishment of common
technical specifications are crucial to ensure interoperability across the
GCC states' defence capabilities.

7. Capacity Building and Human Capital Development:

7.1 Education and Training Programmes:

Developing robust education and training programmes focused on science, technology, engineering, and math (STEM) fields is necessary to build the human capital required for successful technology transfer and self-reliance in the defence industry.

7.2 Collaboration with Academic Institutions and Research Centres:

Engaging with academic and research institutions enhances knowledge exchange, fosters cutting-edge research, and nurtures talent capable of supporting defence industry innovation and technological development.

7.3 Importance of Building a Skilled Workforce:

Developing a skilled workforce equipped with the necessary technical know-how contributes to successfully absorbing and utilising transferred technologies. Investing in training programmes, professional development, and knowledge-sharing platforms strengthens the capacity and competency of the local workforce in defence technology domains.

8. Technological Innovation and R&D:

8.1 Promoting Research and Development Activities:

Encouraging research and development activities enables the GCC states to drive innovation and develop indigenous defence technologies. Through funding, grants, and favourable policy frameworks, government support can stimulate research in key technological areas.

8.2 Encouraging Public-Private Partnerships:

Collaboration between the public and private sectors is vital for fostering technological innovation. Public-private partnerships facilitate sharing resources, expertise, and risk in research and development projects, accelerating the pace of technology transfer and localised defence industry growth.

8.3 Leveraging Defence Industry Clusters and Innovation Hubs:

Establishing defence industry clusters and innovation hubs promotes collaboration, knowledge sharing, efficiency, and technology diffusion. Concentrating defence-related industries in specific regions fosters a conducive ecosystem for technology transfer, spurs innovation, and encourages the growth of local supply chains.

9. Policy Recommendations9. Policy Recommendations:

9.1 Strengthening Legal and Regulatory Frameworks:

Establishing robust legal and regulatory frameworks that protect intellectual property rights, facilitate technology transfer, and ensure compliance with international export control regimes is crucial. Clear guidelines and transparent processes for technology transfer agreements can provide clarity and stability for both technology providers and recipients.

9.2 Encouraging Public-Private Collaboration:

Foster partnerships between the public and private sectors to drive technology transfer and indigenous defence industry development. This can be achieved through initiatives such as joint research and development projects, knowledge-sharing platforms, and funding mechanisms that incentivise collaboration and innovation.

9.3 Supporting Research and Development:

Provide financial incentives and support for research and development activities in key technological areas. This includes increasing funding for defence-related research programmes, establishing grants and scholarships for researchers and students, and promoting collaborations between academia, industry, and government researchers.

9.4 Investing in Education and Skills Development:

Enhance education and training programmes in STEM fields, specifically focusing on defence technology areas. This can be achieved through curriculum development, scholarship programmes, and partnerships with academic institutions and research centres to ensure a continuous pipeline of skilled workforce capable of supporting technology transfer and self-reliance efforts.

9.5 Encouraging Technology Exchange Programmes:

Facilitate technology exchange programmes between the GCC states and technologically advanced nations through initiatives such as internships, training programmes, and collaborative research projects. This enhances knowledge-sharing, exposes local talent to cutting-edge technologies, and fosters a culture of innovation within the defence industry.

9.6 Promoting Defence Industry Clusters:

Create specialised defence industry clusters and innovation hubs that bring together defence companies, research institutions, educational organisations, and relevant support services. These clusters can serve as centres of excellence, promoting collaboration, technology diffusion, and localised supply chain development.

9.7 Establishing Technology Transfer Clearinghouses:

Develop centralised technology transfer clearinghouses that serve as repositories of information, expertise, and best practices in defence technology. These clearinghouses can facilitate knowledge exchange, guide technology transfer processes, and promote networking among stakeholders involved in technology transfer initiatives.

9.8 Strengthening Regional Collaboration:

Encourage collaboration and cooperation between the GCC states in defence technology development and technology transfer initiatives. By pooling resources and sharing knowledge, the GCC states can accelerate their progress towards self-reliance and enhance their regional security capabilities.

9.9 Monitoring and Evaluation:

Establish mechanisms to monitor and evaluate the effectiveness of technology transfer initiatives and their impact on self-reliance in the defence industry. Regular assessments will help identify areas of improvement, address challenges, and ensure that the desired outcomes of technology transfer efforts are achieved.

9.10 Promoting International Cooperation:

Foster international cooperation in defence technology transfer through partnerships, joint research programmes, and participation in international defence exhibitions and conferences. Engaging with technologically advanced nations can facilitate access to advanced defence technologies, expertise, and potential collaboration opportunities.

In conclusion, technology transfer is critical in achieving self-reliance in the defence industry within the GCC states. By pursuing effective technology transfer initiatives, the GCC states can reduce their dependency on foreign sources, enhance their autonomy and national security, foster indigenous technological capabilities, and stimulate economic growth. However, challenges such as technological gaps, intellectual property rights issues, and the need for capacity building and innovation support must be addressed to ensure successful technology transfer and sustainable self-reliance. Implementing comprehensive policies and strategies, along with effective collaborations among government, industry, and academia, will be essential to realise the full potential of technology transfer for defence industry modernisation and self-sufficiency.

Chapter 15

Economic Implications of Indigenisation

*T*he Gulf Cooperation Council (GCC) states have realised the potential *of developing their defence industries within their borders. This will help them to reduce their reliance on foreign arms imports and establish local defence manufacturing capabilities. By doing so, they are aiming to achieve several economic benefits. This chapter delves deeper into the economic implications of indigenisation in the GCC by focusing on job creation, technological innovation, foreign direct investment, and overall economic growth resulting from localised defence industries.*

1. Job Creation and Technological Innovation

Developing localised defence industries in the GCC presents a significant opportunity for job creation. As these countries establish their own defence manufacturing facilities, there is a growing need for a skilled workforce in engineering, manufacturing, research, and design areas. This provides employment opportunities for citizens and reduces dependence on foreign labour. Moreover, as the defence industry requires a highly specialised workforce, job creation in this sector often leads to the development of specialised skills and knowledge that can be transferred to other industries, further enhancing the region's human capital.

Indigenisation also fosters technological innovation within the GCC states. As local defence industries develop, they invest in research and development to meet their defence needs. This investment in innovation leads to the generation of new technologies, which can then be leveraged across other sectors of the economy. For instance, advancements in aerospace technology can have applications in the transportation industry, while developments in communications systems can enhance telecommunications infrastructure. The spillover effect of defence innovations can drive advancements in fields such as robotics, materials science, artificial intelligence, and cybersecurity, thus enhancing the overall competitiveness of the GCC economies.

2. Trickle-Down Technologies and Economic Growth

The growth of localised defence industries in the GCC can positively impact the broader economy, stimulating economic growth and diversification. As defence manufacturing capabilities expand, there is an increased demand for various goods and services, including raw materials, machinery, and components. This creates opportunities for local suppliers and stimulates economic activity in related sectors, increasing investment and job creation. The establishment of defence clusters can attract both domestic and foreign investments, subsequently bolstering the overall economy.

Furthermore, the technological expertise gained through indigenisation can spill over into other sectors, fostering innovation, productivity, and competitiveness. For example, advancements in the defence sector, such as in unmanned aerial systems or cyber defence technologies, can have applications in various non-defence industries like agriculture, infrastructure development, disaster management, and healthcare. The utilisation of such technologies can lead to efficiency gains, cost reductions, and improved quality in these sectors. Additionally, defence expenditures can also act as a catalyst for infrastructural development, such as improving transportation networks and constructing manufacturing facilities, further stimulating economic growth.

3. Foreign Direct Investment and Knowledge Transfer

Pursuing indigenisation in the defence industry can attract foreign direct investment (FDI) to the GCC states. As localised defence industries develop capabilities and reputations, global defence companies may seek collaboration or partnerships to access these emerging markets. This influx of FDI bolsters the financial resources available for defence indigenisation and brings in additional expertise and technologies.

Collaborating with international defence companies can enable knowledge transfer, technology exchange, and skill development as GCC nations work hand-in-hand with established players in the industry. These collaborations can foster the transfer of best practices, cutting-edge technologies, and international networks, accelerating the advancement of local defence industries. Such knowledge transfer can also be leveraged to strengthen and expand non-defence sectors, promoting overall economic diversity and growth.

Case Studies from Israel and Turkey

Case studies from Israel and Turkey provide valuable insights to further explore the potential economic benefits of defence indigenisation and to explore the potential economic benefits of defence indigenisation further.

Both countries have successfully developed and nurtured their defence industries, resulting in significant economic dividends.

Israel's successful defence industry, driven by technological innovation, has played a pivotal role in transforming the country into a global technology powerhouse. Israeli defence companies have gained a reputation for delivering advanced defence and security solutions exported worldwide. This has spurred the growth of a thriving defence industry that has had a multiplier effect on the Israeli economy. High-value jobs have been created, foreign investments have been attracted, and innovation has been fostered in various sectors such as cybersecurity, aerospace, and telecommunications.

Similarly, Turkey's ambitious defence indigenisation programme has enabled the country to enhance its self-sufficiency in defence production. This has reduced Turkey's dependence on foreign suppliers and contributed to economic growth. The defence industry has become a key contributor to Turkey's export revenues, while domestic defence companies have benefited from technology transfer and collaborative ventures with international partners. These economic gains have helped propel Turkey's overall industrial and technological advancements.

By examining the experiences of Israel and Turkey, the GCC states can draw valuable insights and lessons that can inform their own indigenisation strategies. Engaging in comprehensive defence indigenisation programmes can provide the GCC with a pathway to economic development, job creation, technological innovation, and enhanced competitiveness on a global scale.

In conclusion, the economic implications of defence indigenisation in the GCC are substantial. The region can create jobs, foster technological innovation, attract foreign direct investment, and stimulate economic growth by developing local defence industries. Establishing defence clusters and the spillover of defence technologies into other sectors can further amplify these economic benefits. By harnessing the potential of indigenisation, the GCC states can strengthen their economies and build sustainable defence capabilities for the future.

Chapter 16

Job Creation and Technological Innovation

*T*he localisation of the defence industry in the Gulf Cooperation Council *(GCC) states has not only been driven by strategic and autonomy considerations but also holds significant economic implications. One of the key benefits of indigenising the defence industry is the potential for job creation and fostering technological innovation within the region.*

The GCC states can create many job opportunities across various sectors by establishing indigenous defence capabilities. The defence industry requires a broad range of skilled professionals, including engineers, technicians, scientists, and support staff. As these countries invest in developing their defence capabilities, they also invest in their workforce. This means providing specialised training programmes, supporting research and development institutions, and collaborating with educational institutions to ensure a skilled labour force.

The job creation potential extends beyond the direct employment opportunities within the defence industry. Localising the defence industry also spurs the growth of ancillary industries such as manufacturing, logistics, and maintenance and repair services. For example, establishing a domestic defence manufacturing sector requires the production of equipment, vehicles, and systems, which in turn support various supply chains. This not only creates jobs in manufacturing but also fosters the growth of the wider industrial sector.

Furthermore, the growth of the defence industry can have positive multiplier effects on the economy. As defence-related jobs are created, individuals have more disposable income, leading to increased consumption. This increased domestic demand can drive economic growth and stimulate other sectors of the economy, such as retail, hospitality, and services. Additionally, developing the defence industry often requires investment in infrastructure such as research centres, technology parks, and testing facilities. This infrastructure development provides opportunities for construction jobs and indirectly stimulates related industries, such as engineering and architecture.

Establishing local defence industries will provide employment opportunities and attract talent, helping to retain highly skilled individuals within the region. Retention of talent is essential for sustained economic growth and development. By offering competitive salaries and benefits, career advancement opportunities, and a supportive work environment, the defence industry can serve as an anchor for skilled professionals, preventing brain drain and encouraging individuals to contribute their expertise to the local economy.

Moreover, the development and advancement of the defence industry in the GCC states can act as a catalyst for technological innovation. The process of localisation necessitates the acquisition and development of advanced technologies, pushing the boundaries of research and development within these countries. This can lead to breakthroughs in various fields, such as aerospace, cybersecurity, autonomous systems, artificial intelligence, and advanced manufacturing.

The defence industry often acts as a pioneer in adopting cutting-edge technologies. The need for advanced military capabilities drives research and development in areas such as sensor technologies, communications, and propulsion systems. As a result, the defence industry has become a prime source of technological advancements, with potential applications across multiple sectors.

As the defence industry seeks to stay at the cutting edge of technology, it often leads to the creation of spin-off industries and the development of new technologies with civilian applications. The expertise and knowledge gained from defence-focused research and development efforts can be transferred to other sectors, resulting in the emergence of innovative technologies that benefit society as a whole. For example, advancements in materials science, robotics, and communications technology originating from defence research can find applications in healthcare, infrastructure development, and transportation.

Trickle-down technologies also play a crucial role in driving economic growth. As the defence industry develops and integrates advanced technologies, the resultant expertise and knowledge spill over to other industries, leading to the rapid development of related sectors. For instance, using advanced materials in defence manufacturing can enhance automotive manufacturing processes, resulting in lighter and more fuel-efficient vehicles. The digital communication systems developed for military applications can be adapted to improve civilian telecommunications networks. This cross-pollination of technologies translates into improved efficiency, increased productivity, and enhanced competitiveness of the defence sector and the broader economy.

Additionally, the localisation of the defence industry fosters research and development collaboration between local and international entities. The GCC states often engage in partnerships, joint ventures, and technology transfers with international defence companies to achieve self-sufficiency in defence capabilities. These collaborations provide knowledge exchange, technology transfer, and capacity-building opportunities. As local entities collaborate with international firms, they acquire state-of-the-art technology, gain exposure to best practices, and develop a deeper understanding of global defence industry standards.

Case studies from other countries, such as Israel and Turkey, can be examined to draw insights into the economic implications of indigenisation efforts. Israel, for example, has successfully leveraged its defence industry to become a global leader in innovative technologies, particularly in the fields of cybersecurity and unmanned systems. This has bolstered the Israeli economy and positioned the country as a sought-after partner for collaborations and defence exports, leading to a robust defence technology ecosystem.

Similarly, Turkey's defence industry has experienced significant growth, resulting in job creation, technology transfer, and increased defence exports. The development of indigenous defence capabilities has enhanced Turkey's national security and contributed to its economic growth by creating jobs and spurring technological innovation. Turkey's success in the defence sector has established it as a regional hub for research and development and as a major player in global defence exports.

In conclusion, the localisation of the defence industry in the GCC states has the potential to generate employment opportunities and stimulate technological innovation. Beyond the immediate defence sector, the establishment of indigenous capabilities can have far-reaching economic implications, leading to the growth of related industries and the region's overall development. The successful examples of other countries, such as Israel and Turkey, can serve as valuable lessons and provide insights for the GCC states as they embark on their journey towards creating a vibrant and technologically advanced defence industry. By investing in the necessary infrastructure and human capital, these countries can establish themselves as hubs of innovation and contribute to the broader socioeconomic development of the region.

Chapter 17

Trickle-Down Technologies and Economic Growth

In recent years, the localisation of defence industries within the Gulf Co-operation Council (GCC) states has led to a significant shift in economic dynamics. It has become increasingly apparent that developing indigenous defence capabilities is crucial for national security and holds substantial potential for driving economic growth and creating employment opportunities. This chapter explores the concept of "trickle-down technologies" and examines its correlation with economic growth in the context of the GCC defence industry localisation.

One of the key benefits of developing a localised defence industry is the creation of high-skilled jobs. As GCC states work towards developing their defence capabilities, they are simultaneously investing in research and development, innovation, and the acquisition of advanced technologies. This process requires specialised expertise and provides opportunities for local talent acquisition, nurturing a highly skilled workforce in various scientific, technical, and engineering fields. The resulting job creation has a direct and positive impact on economic growth since it increases the income and spending power of individuals, which, in turn, stimulates consumer demand and invigorates domestic industries.

Furthermore, the localisation of defence industries allows for knowledge transfer and technology diffusion. When international defence companies collaborate with local firms or establish joint ventures, they often bring advanced technologies, manufacturing processes, and know-how that can be transferred to the local workforce and industry. This knowledge is then absorbed by the local defence companies and subsequently spills over into other sectors of the economy, leading to the emergence of new industries and the improvement of existing ones.

The process of technology diffusion in the defence sector can have a profound impact on economic growth. Firstly, it enhances overall productivity by enabling companies to streamline their processes, automate tasks, and improve efficiency. This improved efficiency translates into cost savings, which can be reinvested in expanding production, hiring more employees, or investing in research and development activities. Secondly, technology diffusion promotes competitiveness by enabling local defence companies to deliver products and services that meet international standards. This enhances their ability to compete in global markets and attract foreign investments.

In addition to these direct economic impacts, the concept of trickle-down technologies in the defence industry also extends to indirect benefits. As indigenous defence industries flourish, they have the potential to stimulate the growth of a local supply chain. When local defence companies seek to meet the demands of their projects, they often collaborate with local suppliers, subcontractors, and service providers. This collaboration creates a multiplier effect within the economy, as it not only generates additional employment opportunities but also increases demand for goods and services in related industries, such as raw materials, transportation, logistics, and professional services.

The stimulation of the local supply chain brings about several advantages. Firstly, it reduces dependence on imports and fosters economic self-sufficiency. As local suppliers develop capabilities to meet the requirements of the defence industry, the reliance on foreign suppliers diminishes, leading to a more balanced and sustainable economy. Secondly, the growth of the local supply chain increases resilience and reduces vulnerability to external shocks. By developing local manufacturing capabilities and strengthening ties with domestic suppliers, defence companies can mitigate the risks associated with fluctuations in global supply chains, ensuring a steady availability of critical components and materials.

However, establishing a localised defence industry requires a holistic approach encompassing various elements of economic development. Education and research infrastructure play vital roles in building a knowledge-based economy capable of sustaining advanced defence industries. Investment in education, particularly in STEM (science, technology, engineering, and mathematics), is essential to develop a skilled workforce that can effectively contribute to defence-related research, design, and production. Additionally, establishing research institutes and universities dedicated to defence-related research fosters innovation and paves the way for breakthrough technologies with wide-ranging applicability beyond the defence sector.

Furthermore, collaboration between academia, industry, and government is crucial to accelerate the development of indigenous technologies. Partnerships that facilitate knowledge exchange, joint research projects, and technology incubation platforms support the creation of an innovation ecosystem that drives economic growth and technological advancement. Such collaboration allows universities and research institutions to align their research projects and educational programmes with the needs of the defence industry, enhancing the practical applicability of the knowledge generated.

Moreover, the localisation of defence industries can have significant spillover effects regarding skill development and entrepreneurship. As local defence companies gain access to advanced technologies and knowledge, employees and entrepreneurs within these companies acquire valuable skills and expertise. This creates a pool of human capital that can potentially fuel innovation and create spin-off businesses in related industries. The presence of a vibrant defence industry ecosystem can attract talented individuals, foster a culture of innovation, and create a favourable environment for startups and entrepreneurship.

Another aspect to consider in the context of trickle-down technologies is the impact on research and development (R&D) capabilities. Establishing indigenous defence industries necessitates investments in R&D infrastructure, laboratories, and testing facilities. These investments not only support defence-specific research but also contribute to a nation's overall scientific and technological capabilities. As the defence industry evolves and generates demand for cutting-edge technologies, R&D activities will expand beyond defence applications and find relevance in various sectors, such as aerospace, telecommunications, and energy.

Furthermore, developing a localised defence industry can align with broader national economic diversification strategies. By focusing on building defence capabilities, countries can simultaneously address their security needs and reduce reliance on traditional revenue sources, such as oil and gas. The defence industry presents an opportunity to diversify the economy and create sustainable growth by leveraging existing expertise and resources. This diversification also enhances resilience by creating a more balanced economy that is less susceptible to price fluctuations and geopolitical uncertainties.

To ensure the long-term success of defence industry localisation, governments must adopt policies and strategies that promote innovation, entrepreneurship, and the creation of an enabling business environment. This includes providing financial incentives for research and development activities, facilitating access to venture capital, and creating mechanisms to protect intellectual property rights. Investing in infrastructure development, such as industrial parks or innovation hubs, can attract local and foreign companies, driving further economic growth and fostering collaboration between industry players.

In conclusion, developing localised defence industries in the GCC states offers substantial opportunities for economic growth by generating high-skilled jobs, facilitating knowledge transfer, fostering technological diffusion, and stimulating the growth of local supply chains. Trickle-down technologies resulting from defence industry localisation have the potential to drive overall economic development, diversification, and resilience. By recognising the broader economic implications of the defence sector, policymakers can leverage this potential to create sustainable economic growth and enhance the technological capabilities of their countries. A comprehensive approach that combines investments in education, research infrastructure, and collaborations between academia, industry, and government will be crucial in realising these benefits and ensuring long-term economic prosperity.

Chapter 18

Case Studies from Israel and Turkey

To further understand the economic implications of the indigenisation of the defence industry, it is important to examine case studies from countries that have successfully developed their own defence capabilities. Two notable examples are Israel and Turkey.

Israel has long been known for its strong defence industry, which has played a crucial role in its security and economic development. With limited natural resources and surrounded by hostile neighbours, Israel recognised the need to develop its own defence capabilities early on. Israel has successfully developed cutting-edge defence technologies through heavy investment in research and development, technology transfer, and close collaboration between academia and the private sector.

One of the key factors behind Israel's successful indigenisation of the defence industry is its emphasis on innovation. The country has fostered a culture of entrepreneurship and creativity, encouraging its defence companies to think outside the box and develop unique solutions to complex problems. This has led to the creation of world-class defence technologies that are in high demand globally.

Israel has also benefitted from its close collaboration with the military.

The Israeli Defence Forces (IDF) have played an active role in shaping the country's defence industry by providing feedback, requirements, and even funding for research and development projects. This close partnership between the military and the defence industry has ensured that the technologies developed are tailored to the specific needs of the Israeli armed forces, making them more efficient and effective.

Furthermore, Israel has leveraged its strong ties with the United States to enhance its defence capabilities. The U.S. has been a key supplier of military aid, providing Israel with advanced weaponry, equipment, and training. This partnership has strengthened Israel's security and facilitated technology transfer and knowledge sharing, enabling Israeli defence companies to learn from the best practices of U.S. defence contractors.

The indigenisation of the defence industry in Israel has not only bolstered the country's security but has also had significant economic benefits. The defence sector is a major contributor to Israel's exports, generating substantial revenues and creating high-skilled job opportunities. Moreover, advancements in defence technologies have found civilian applications, leading to the growth of dual-use industries such as cybersecurity, telecommunication, and medical devices. These spin-off industries have further boosted the economy, attracting domestic and foreign investments.

On the other hand, Turkey embarked on a similar journey to develop its defence industry in the 1980s. Facing regional conflicts and external pressure, Turkey sought to reduce its dependency on foreign defence suppliers and achieve self-sufficiency. The Turkish defence industry has since made significant progress, particularly in producing armoured vehicles, naval vessels, and aerospace technologies.

Turkey implemented a series of strategic policies and investments to achieve a successful indigenisation process. The country established defence research and development agencies, collaborated with international partners for technology transfer, and provided financial incentives to local defence companies. This comprehensive approach led to the growth of a robust defence industry in Turkey.

The economic impact of defence industry indigenisation in Turkey has been substantial. The sector has experienced rapid growth and has become a key contributor to the country's GDP. The development of the domestic defence industry has created employment opportunities and resulted in technology transfer agreements with international partners. Turkey's defence exports have increased and diversified, reaching many countries worldwide. Furthermore, Turkey has utilised its defence capabilities for export, enhancing its global standing and generating much-needed revenue.

Turkey's success in indigenisation can also be attributed to its focus on research and development. The country has established defence technology centres, innovation clusters, and research institutes to foster technological growth within the defence industry. This emphasis on innovation has allowed Turkey to develop advanced defence technologies that are on par with global standards.

Additionally, Turkey has actively pursued joint ventures and collaborations to develop critical defence technologies. By partnering with international companies, Turkey has gained access to expertise, know-how, and advanced technologies that have accelerated its defence industry's growth. This approach has not only boosted the capabilities of Turkish defence companies but has also facilitated technology transfer, paving the way for increased self-reliance and indigenous production.

The case studies of Israel and Turkey indicate that the indigenisation of the defence industry can have significant economic benefits. Both countries have successfully leveraged their defence capabilities to foster technological innovation, create jobs, and enhance economic growth. These examples inspire the Gulf Cooperation Council (GCC) states as they strive to localise their defence industries and boost their economies.

By examining and learning from these case studies, the GCC states can gain valuable insights into the strategies, policies, and investments necessary for achieving a successful indigenisation process. However, it is crucial to acknowledge the unique regional dynamics. It challenges the GCC states face, which may require tailored approaches and adaptations to capitalise on the economic potential of their defence industries fully.

In conclusion, the case studies of Israel and Turkey demonstrate that the defence industry's indigenisation can catalyse economic growth and technological advancement. These countries have transformed their defence sectors into major economic contributors, attracting investments, creating employment opportunities, and boosting exports. The lessons learnt from these case studies can guide other nations in localising their defence industries, ensuring national security and economic prosperity. The indigenisation of the defence industry holds great potential for countries seeking to strengthen their defence capabilities and enhance their economic development.

Chapter 19

Implications for Gulf Regional Security

*T*he localisation of the defence industry in the Gulf Cooperation Council (GCC) states holds profound and multifaceted implications for Gulf regional security, reshaping the future trajectory of the region's geopolitical landscape. This transformation marks a strategic shift towards reducing vulnerabilities, enhancing resilience, recalibrating alliances, and fostering indigenous defence capabilities, which converge to create a holistic and self-reliant security framework.

Firstly, reducing vulnerabilities becomes a paramount objective for the GCC states through the localisation of the defence industry. Historically, these states heavily relied on external suppliers, leaving them vulnerable to geopolitical disruptions and potential arms embargoes. Notable events, such as the Iran-Iraq War and the Gulf War, exposed the vulnerabilities of relying on external sources for defence equipment and technologies. By developing indigenous defence manufacturing capabilities, the GCC states mitigate these vulnerabilities and enhance their capacity to protect their national interests. This increased self-sufficiency ensures a continuous supply of vital defence equipment and fortifies their ability to respond effectively to emerging security challenges, reducing their dependence on external actors.

Moreover, the localisation of the defence industry serves as a crucial pillar for enhancing the resilience of the GCC states in the face of regional security threats. Complex security dynamics, including territorial disputes, regional rivalries, terrorism, and emerging non-state actors, characterise the Gulf region. These challenges demand flexible and agile defence capabilities that can swiftly adapt to evolving circumstances. By reducing their reliance on foreign suppliers and fostering local expertise, the GCC states can develop defence systems that are tailored to their specific needs, ensuring quick responses to emerging threats. Furthermore, localised defence industries allow for better coordination and collaboration among the GCC states in times of crisis, enhancing their collective resilience and bolstering regional security across the Gulf.

Localisation also brings forth the imperative of recalibrating alliances and power dynamics in the Gulf region. As the GCC states develop their own defence capabilities, their reliance on traditional partners, notably the United States, may gradually shift. While existing security partnerships will remain important, the GCC states may seek to diversify their defence sources and forge more balanced and mutually beneficial partnerships. This recalibration of alliances could foster increased regional cooperation while granting the GCC states greater autonomy in decision-making processes related to defence strategies and responses. The evolving dynamics in defence collaboration may lead to the emergence of new regional security configurations, impacting the overall balance of power in the Gulf region.

The long-term prospects of local defence industries also bear implications for regional security. As the GCC states nurture domestic defence manufacturing capabilities, they incentivise technological advancements, research, and innovation in the defence sector. This fosters a continuous improvement cycle, allowing for the acquisition of cutting-edge military technologies and expertise. Gulf states can maintain a competitive edge in defence capabilities by establishing research and development centres, investing in innovation, and encouraging collaboration with academia and private sectors. As they become self-reliant in the production of defence equipment and systems, the GCC states can enhance their deterrence posture, contributing to the overall security and stability of the region.

Furthermore, the localisation of the defence industry facilitates closer integration of defence strategies among the GCC states, paving the way for enhanced collective defence capabilities. Collaborative research, development, and production efforts can lead to joint defence projects, cooperative military ventures, and even the formation of a common defence architecture. This convergence strengthens the solidarity among the GCC states and ensures a more cohesive approach to addressing common security challenges. The GCC states can effectively deter potential adversaries and project stability and security throughout the Gulf region by pooling resources, sharing defence technologies, and coordinating military doctrines and exercises.

Additionally, the localisation of the defence industry generates significant socio-economic benefits for the GCC countries. The establishment and growth of local defence industries create job opportunities and stimulate economic diversification, reducing their reliance on oil revenues. The defence sector acts as a catalyst for technology transfer, encouraging the development of a knowledge-based economy and fostering innovation in other industries. The defence industry's contribution to economic diversification enhances the overall resilience of the GCC states' economies. It lays the groundwork for sustainable development and the transformation of their national industries in the long run.

In conclusion, the localisation of the defence industry in the GCC states carries profound and transformative implications for Gulf regional security. The GCC states are signalling a strategic shift towards a holistic and self-reliant security framework by reducing vulnerabilities, enhancing resilience, recalibrating alliances, and fostering indigenous defence capabilities. This transformation not only bolsters the GCC states' autonomy, adaptability, and deterrence capabilities but also promotes stability, prosperity, and resilience throughout the Gulf region.

Chapter 20

Reducing Vulnerabilities and Enhancing Resilience

*G*iven the evolving geopolitical landscape and regional security concerns, it is crucial for the Gulf Cooperation Council (GCC) states to focus on developing a local defence industry. This strategic objective is aimed at reducing vulnerabilities and enhancing resilience. This chapter will explore the various aspects and benefits of these efforts.

One of the key vulnerabilities that the GCC states currently face is their heavy reliance on foreign defence equipment and technology. This over-dependence on external suppliers exposes them to potential risks of supply chain disruptions and leaves them susceptible to export control restrictions, geopolitical tensions, and shifting alliances. Consequently, reducing this dependency becomes crucial for bolstering security and ensuring the autonomy of the GCC states in shaping their defence capabilities.

Localisation efforts focus on building domestic defence manufacturing capabilities to tackle this vulnerability effectively. By establishing indigenous defence industries, the GCC states can reduce their external dependencies and create a robust industrial base that promotes economic growth and job creation. This industrial growth is not limited to defence alone but often spills over into other sectors, leading to diversification and the development of high-tech industries that contribute to long-term sustainability.

Key considerations in the localisation process include fostering technology transfer, enhancing research and development capacities, and building strategic alliances with international defence firms. Technology transfer agreements enable the acquisition of critical knowledge and expertise, allowing GCC states to enhance local production capabilities and reduce reliance on foreign suppliers. These agreements can take various forms, including collaborative research and development projects, joint ventures, licencing agreements, and acquiring intellectual property rights. By tailoring these agreements to meet specific needs, the GCC states can capitalise on the expertise of foreign partners while safeguarding their own strategic interests.

Strategic partnerships with leading defence companies further facilitate the transfer of advanced technologies, knowledge sharing, and joint development projects, ultimately bolstering the indigenous defence industry's capabilities. These partnerships go beyond mere supplier-customer relationships, often involving joint investments and ventures, enabling the GCC states to access cutting-edge technologies and gain insights into industry best practices. These alliances also enhance the credibility and reputation of the GCC defence industry, attracting further investments and international collaborations.

In addition to reducing vulnerabilities, localisation efforts enhance resilience in multiple ways. First and foremost, building local defence industries increases the self-sufficiency and flexibility of the GCC states in responding to security threats. A diversified defence industrial base enables the rapid development and deployment of tailored solutions that align with the specific needs and challenges faced by the region. By controlling their defence production, the GCC states can quickly adapt to emerging threats, such as cyber warfare, unconventional warfare, and hybrid threats, which continue to evolve in complexity and sophistication.

Moreover, investing in local defence manufacturing capabilities promotes the growth of a highly skilled workforce. The defence industry becomes an engine of socio-economic development by providing employment opportunities for engineers, scientists, technicians, and skilled labourers. Specialised training programmes and educational initiatives can be established to meet the industry's specific workforce needs, ensuring a steady supply of competent professionals. Not only does this bolster the local workforce, but it also reduces unemployment rates, alleviates socio-economic disparities, and fosters social stability. Overall, improved economic conditions contribute to national resilience and strengthen the social fabric of the GCC states.

Furthermore, localisation efforts ensure the deep integration of the defence industry with other sectors, such as academia, research institutions, and innovative startups. Collaborative and interdisciplinary approaches enable the development of cutting-edge technologies, leading to advancements across various sectors, including telecommunications, electronics, aerospace, and advanced materials. By fostering an innovation and knowledge exchange ecosystem, the GCC states can tap into the intellectual capital and resources available domestically and globally. The resulting spillover effects foster a culture of innovation, attracting international collaboration and investment and positioning the GCC states as regional centres of excellence in defence and technology.

Beyond the economic and security benefits, localisation in the defence industry also has geopolitical implications. The development of autonomous capabilities reduces the reliance on external powers for defence needs, providing the GCC states with greater autonomy in crafting their foreign policy and strategic alignments. This newfound independence empowers these states to adopt more assertive roles and take proactive measures to promote regional stability, mediate conflicts, and contribute to collective security efforts. A strong domestic defence industry can also become a source of soft power. GCC countries can supply advanced defence equipment and technology to other nations, building strategic partnerships and alliances based on mutual interests.

In conclusion, the localisation of the defence industry in the GCC states serves as an essential tool for reducing vulnerabilities and enhancing resilience. By building indigenous defence manufacturing capabilities, fostering technological advancements, and strengthening research and development capacities, the GCC states can decrease their dependence on foreign suppliers, promote economic growth, and bolster their security. Furthermore, localisation efforts contribute to regional stability, foster socio-economic development, and position these states as key players in the global defence industry. Strategic partnerships, technology transfer, and fostering a skilled workforce further further their capabilities on both domestic and international levels, ensuring autonomy and adaptive responses to emerging security challenges. Ultimately, localisation is a comprehensive approach that enhances the security of the GCC states and strengthens their position in the global arena.

Chapter 21

Recalibrating Alliances and Power Dynamics

The ongoing process of localisation in the defence industry of the Gulf Cooperation Council (GCC) states has ushered in a new era of alliances and power dynamics within the region. As these states endeavour to attain greater self-reliance and reduce their external dependencies, they must reevaluate their defence partnerships and alliances with traditional suppliers. This recalibration process entails numerous factors, intricacies, and considerations that significantly shape the future of the region's defence landscape.

The GCC states have relied heavily on the United States as their primary defence supplier and strategic partner. This alliance ensured access to advanced military hardware, technology, and training while providing a security guarantee against external threats. However, the push towards localisation has instigated a notable shift in the dynamics of these alliances.

Developing local defence industries has resulted in declining arms imports from traditional suppliers. The GCC states' efforts to produce their own defence equipment stem from a fundamental belief that self-sufficiency enhances national security. By diminishing their reliance on foreign arms suppliers, these countries aim to safeguard their defence capabilities even during periods of political uncertainty or arms embargoes.

However, the localisation of defence industries is not a straightforward endeavour. Constructing a sustainable defence industrial base demands substantial investments in infrastructure development, research and development capabilities, and skilled human resources. Moreover, acquiring the necessary technology and know-how can prove challenging, particularly in sensitive areas such as aerospace, naval vessels, or advanced weapon systems.

To overcome these challenges, GCC states have pursued diverse strategies. Some have sought partnerships with established defence manufacturers, leveraging joint ventures to facilitate technology transfer and co-production. This approach benefits both parties, providing the GCC states access to advanced technologies while allowing the original suppliers to expand their market reach and enhance competitiveness.

In recent years, significant progress has been witnessed in the localisation efforts of countries like Saudi Arabia and the United Arab Emirates (UAE). Saudi Arabia's Vision 2030 plan encompasses a comprehensive agenda for industrial diversification, aiming to localise 50% of its military spending by 2030. Meanwhile, established companies such as EDGE exemplify the UAE's commitment to developing an advanced defence industry, which focuses on domestically developing critical defence technologies.

The emergence of robust local defence industries also transforms the balance of power within the region. GCC states that it can develop advanced defence capabilities and consequently gain a degree of influence and leverage in regional security matters. This alteration in power dynamics can lead to shifts in regional alliances and reconfiguration of political partnerships.

For instance, the UAE has steadily increased its defence capabilities and become an influential player in the regional security landscape. Its active involvement in military interventions, such as in Yemen and Libya, showcases this growing influence. Similarly, Qatar's investments in defence research and development have enabled the nation to enhance its military capabilities, expanding its diplomatic and security engagement within the region.

Furthermore, the localisation of the defence industry in GCC states holds broader geopolitical implications. As these states gain greater self-reliance in defence, they may seek to assert their own interests and agendas more independently on the global stage. This could potentially lead to realignments in alliances and partnerships and changes in resource allocation and strategic priorities.

For instance, Saudi Arabia's Vision 2030 plan, in addition to its localisation goals, stresses the importance of diversifying its economy. By reducing its dependence on oil revenues and investing in sectors like defence manufacturing and technology, Saudi Arabia aims to become a global investment powerhouse. This economic diversification and enhanced defence capabilities can significantly impact the kingdom's regional and global influence.

Beyond the immediate region, the localisation of the defence industry in the GCC states may unleash ripple effects on the global defence trade. As these states become formidable players in the defence manufacturing sector, they have the potential to disrupt established arms markets and influence the profitability of major arms-producing countries.

Moreover, the shift towards localised defence industries in the GCC states presents opportunities for collaboration and partnerships with other nations, particularly those striving to diversify their own defence supply chains. Western arms suppliers, such as the United States and European countries, are increasingly inclined to engage in technology transfers and joint development ventures with the GCC states. This mutually beneficial engagement can foster innovation, create new markets, and contribute to economic growth for all parties involved.

In conclusion, the process of localising the defence industry in the GCC states has multifaceted implications for alliances and power dynamics. It necessitates strategic considerations as countries balance their aspirations for self-sufficiency and maintain productive defence partnerships. The emergence of robust local defence industries can reshape regional power dynamics and have wide-ranging geopolitical consequences. It is crucial for the GCC states to navigate these changes skillfully, ensuring national security while positively contributing to regional and global stability.

Chapter 22

The Role of Local Defence Industries in Future Prospects

The Gulf Cooperation Council (GCC) states have strongly emphasised localising their defence industries in recent years. This chapter provides an in-depth analysis of the role of local defence industries in shaping the future prospects of the GCC countries.

One of the primary objectives of developing local defence industries is to enhance the self-sufficiency and autonomy of the GCC states in meeting their defence requirements. These countries seek to minimise vulnerabilities and enhance their national security posture by reducing their dependence on foreign suppliers. The ability to produce their own defence equipment ensures a reliable supply chain, decreases reliance on external factors, and allows for flexibility and prompt response during times of crisis.

Local defence industries also play a crucial role in technology transfer and self-reliance. The GCC states aim to acquire the knowledge, skills, and technologies required for indigenisation through partnerships and collaborations with international defence companies. This ensures the adaptation of cutting-edge defence technologies and contributes to the overall growth and diversification of the national economy. Technology transfer can develop a highly skilled workforce and encourage innovation in other sectors, creating a ripple effect of economic progress.

Furthermore, the development of local defence industries has significant economic implications. It can create numerous job opportunities and stimulate technological innovation within the GCC states. The defence industry's contribution to job creation, infrastructure development, and technological advancements can have a multiplier effect on the overall economic growth in the region. Governments in the GCC are actively investing in research and development, establishing defence-focused educational institutions, and encouraging entrepreneurship in the defence sector to harness the economic potential of local defence industries fully.

To comprehensively understand the role of local defence industries, it is essential to examine case studies from countries such as Israel and Turkey. These countries have successfully capitalised on developing their local defence industries, leveraging their defence capabilities to drive economic growth, foreign investment, and exports of defence products and services. Establishing strong local defence industries has allowed these countries to become exporters of defence equipment, generating substantial revenues and driving their technological advancement further.

Israel, in particular, is a notable example of the positive economic impact of local defence industries. With a strong focus on research and development, Israel has met its defence needs and emerged as a global leader in defence technology innovation. Israeli defence companies are known for their expertise in areas such as cybersecurity, unmanned systems, and advanced weaponry. Through exporting its defence products, Israel has significantly contributed to its national economy, boosted employment rates, and attracted foreign investments.

Turkey's experience developing local defence industries showcases the potential for economic growth and technological advancement. The Turkish defence industry has expanded rapidly, focusing on producing a wide range of defence equipment, including armoured vehicles, naval vessels, and aerospace technology. This growth has allowed Turkey to meet its own defence needs and positioned it as a competitive player in the global defence market. The Turkish defence industry has successfully exported its products to various countries, contributing to economic growth, diplomatic relations, and technological cooperation.

On the regional security front, localising defence industries can reduce vulnerabilities and enhance resilience against external threats. When the GCC states can produce their own defence equipment, they become less dependent on imports and potential disruptions in the global supply chain. This increased self-sufficiency can play a critical role in ensuring the security and stability of the region. Moreover, local defence industries provide the opportunity to tailor defence products and technologies to specific regional requirements and challenges, further strengthening their effectiveness in addressing threats to regional security.

Moreover, the localisation of defence industries has geopolitical ramifications both within the region and beyond. As the GCC states develop their defence industries, it can alter power dynamics and reconfigure alliances in the Middle East. The growing capabilities of the local defence industries may impact military cooperation and collaboration with traditional defence partners, leading to new geopolitical alignments and influence. For instance, emerging defence industries in the GCC may compete with and cooperate with established global defence players, shaping the regional and global defence landscape in unforeseen ways.

Furthermore, the localisation of defence industries has implications for global defence trade. As the GCC states develop their capabilities, they may enter the international defence market as suppliers, competing with established industries. This competition can lead to a rebalancing of global defence trade and influence the overall dynamics of the defence industry worldwide. The GCC countries can potentially become vital players in the global defence sector, offering a range of products and services that cater to the unique requirements of their regional and international partners.

In conclusion, the development of local defence industries plays a critical role in shaping the future prospects of the GCC states. It enhances their self-sufficiency, technological capabilities, and economic growth. Additionally, it contributes to regional security and has broader geopolitical and economic implications. The localisation of defence industries can reshape the regional security landscape and influence global defence dynamics. As the GCC states continue down this path, navigating the opportunities and challenges that lie ahead is crucial, ensuring long-term sustainability and maximising the benefits derived from localising their defence industries.

Chapter 23

Geopolitical Ramifications of GCC Defence Industry Localisation

*T*he localisation of the defence industry in the GCC states has significant geopolitical ramifications, both within the region and beyond. Establishing local defence industries shifts power dynamics, influencing the balance of power among Gulf countries and potentially impacting the broader global geopolitical landscape. This chapter explores the multifaceted consequences of GCC defence industry localisation.

Firstly, the localisation of defence industries in the GCC states alters the regional power dynamics in the Arabian Gulf. Traditionally, the United States and other major powers have played a crucial role in shaping the region's security architecture through arms exports and military cooperation. However, the growing self-reliance and development of defence capabilities within the GCC states challenge this historical dynamic. The GCC countries aim to reduce their dependence on external powers for defence equipment and technology by establishing their own defence industries. This newfound autonomy grants them greater flexibility and agency in decision-making processes related to national defence, enabling them to pursue their own strategic goals while potentially reducing their vulnerability to external interference in security affairs.

Moreover, the localisation of the defence industry has implications for the broader global geopolitics. The Gulf region's strategic significance is rooted in its abundant energy resources, geographical location at the crossroads of major trading routes, and its role in shaping the stability of the Middle East. As the GCC states develop their own defence industries, they acquire the capacity to project military power beyond their borders. This raises questions about the possibility of increased assertiveness in regional dynamics and the potential for the GCC states to emerge as major players in the global defence market.

Regarding regional dynamics, the localisation of defence industries may shift the balance of power among the GCC states themselves. Some Gulf countries have historically relied heavily on others for their defence needs, creating dependencies and imbalances. However, as the localisation process progresses, the defence capabilities of different GCC states may increasingly converge, potentially narrowing the gaps between them. This convergence could mitigate the existing power disparities and foster a more balanced distribution of military capabilities within the region.

Localising defence industries in the GCC states also has global implications for trade and arms sales. Historically, the GCC states have been major importers of defence equipment, particularly from the United States and other Western countries. However, with the development of their own defence industries, the dynamics of the global defence trade may transform. The GCC states may become exporters of defence equipment, competing with established defence industries in Europe, the United States, and elsewhere. This shift could lead to increased competition, revised regional security dynamics, and potential changes in diplomatic relations and strategic alliances. Moreover, the improved capabilities of GCC defence industries might also expand the demand for their products beyond the region, resulting in new trade partnerships and diversification of markets.

In addition to these geopolitical ramifications, the localisation of the defence industry in the GCC states has the potential to impact regional and international relations. As GCC countries develop their own defence capabilities, they may seek closer collaborations and partnerships with other major regional actors, such as Turkey, Israel, and Pakistan, which have their respective defence industries. Deeper engagement with these countries could reshape the region's geopolitical dynamics, potentially leading to the formation of new alliances and the realignment of existing ones. These partnerships could strengthen defence cooperation and economic and political ties, thus influencing wider regional stability and global power configurations.

Furthermore, the localisation of defence industries brings socio-economic benefits for GCC countries. The GCC states aim to diversify their economies and reduce their reliance on oil revenues by establishing defence production capabilities. The defence sector could catalyse technological development, innovation, and job creation, leading to the growth of high-skilled employment opportunities for their citizens. As a result, the growth of the defence industry may contribute to political stability and social cohesion within the GCC states.

Another significant consequence of GCC defence industry localisation is its potential impact on indigenous technological advancements and research and development capabilities. As GCC states build their defence industries, they will likely invest in R&D and technological innovation to enhance their defence capabilities. This may lead to the emergence of local expertise in areas such as aerospace engineering, advanced weapon systems, and cybersecurity. Developing indigenous defence technology can have broader implications for national security, strengthening the ability to protect sensitive infrastructure and respond to emerging threats.

Moreover, with increased defence infrastructure and local military production, the GCC states may experience a surge in their defence budgets. This sizable investment in defence can create ripple effects within their economies, stimulating economic growth, driving innovation, and attracting foreign direct investment. Therefore, the defence industry's expansion can play a significant role in economic diversification efforts and transitioning these countries from oil-dependent economies to more sustainable models.

Additionally, the localisation of the defence industry may create interdependencies among the GCC states themselves. Collaboration in defence manufacturing and joint development of defence technology may foster deeper regional integration. This alignment, supported by shared defence constructs and standardised military equipment, could lay the groundwork for stronger military cooperation and defence alliances among the GCC countries. This intra-regional defence integration can enhance collective security and enable coordinated responses to common security challenges.

Lastly, the localisation of the defence industry has implications for Gulf countries' human capital development. Establishing defence industries necessitates cultivating a skilled workforce proficient in various aspects of defence manufacturing, engineering, and research. Governments may invest heavily in education and training programmes to equip their citizens with the necessary skills, fostering a new generation of highly qualified professionals in defence technology. This intentional investment in human capital serves defence purposes. It nurtures talent that can contribute to progression in other sectors, acting as a catalyst for broad-based technological advancement and scientific innovation.

In conclusion, localising the defence industry in the GCC states has far-reaching geopolitical ramifications. It disrupts traditional power dynamics in the region, empowers the GCC countries with increased autonomy and projection of military power, alters the global defence trade landscape, influences regional and international relations, brings socio-economic benefits, fosters indigenous technological advancements, drives economic growth and diversification, strengthens regional integration, and promotes human capital development. Understanding and studying these geopolitical implications are vital for policymakers, defence officials, and strategic thinkers as they navigate the evolving security dynamics in the Gulf region and beyond.

Chapter 24

Influence on Power Dynamics in the Region and Beyond

The localisation of the defence industry within the GCC states has brought about a profound transformation in power dynamics, both within the region and beyond. By developing their own indigenous defence capabilities, these nations have undergone a shift in the balance of power among regional actors, influencing security landscapes across borders.

One of the most significant effects of localised defence industries is the gradual reduction of external dependencies on foreign powers for military equipment and technologies. The GCC states have relied heavily on arms imports from major global powers such as the United States, European countries, and Russia. While these procurements served their defence needs, they also created vulnerabilities and limited their autonomy in decision-making processes. However, with their defence industries' continuous growth and advancement, the GCC states have been steadily freeing themselves from these dependencies, thereby achieving greater strategic autonomy.

The development and expansion of local defence industries have also contributed to the reshaping of alliances and power dynamics within the region. Traditionally, the GCC states had aligned themselves with various global powers based on their defence procurement relationships. However, with the rise of their own defence industries, these states are gaining greater leverage in negotiations and diversifying their partnerships.

This shift in power dynamics has broad implications for regional and international relations. As the GCC states become more self-reliant in defence production, they can increasingly project their influence and assert their interests regionally and globally. At a regional level, localised defence industries enhance GCC states' capabilities to protect their territories, deter potential threats, and play a more assertive role in shaping regional security affairs. This ultimately affects the balance of power among neighbouring countries, potentially leading to new alignments and security arrangements.

The localisation of the defence industry also has economic implications. Establishing local defence industries has created significant job opportunities, boosting employment rates and stimulating economic growth. A skilled workforce is developed through training, research, and innovation, fostering a knowledge-based economy. This shift towards self-sufficiency in defence production has led to the formation of defence industrial complexes encompassing not only manufacturing but also research and development, technology transfer, and support services. These complexes generate a ripple effect on allied sectors, fuelling the growth of related industries such as cybersecurity, aerospace, and high-tech manufacturing.

Moreover, the geopolitical ramifications of the localisation of the defence industry transcend the GCC region. With the GCC states steadily developing their own military technologies and capabilities, they are becoming important players in the global defence trade. The emergence of GCC defence industries can potentially disrupt established global defence markets and challenge the dominance of traditional arms suppliers. This shift not only reshapes global power dynamics but also contributes to the emergence of a multipolar world order.

Furthermore, establishing localised defence industries enables the GCC states to enhance their technological and innovation capabilities. By investing in research and development, they can harness cutting-edge technologies and contribute to advancements in the defence sector. This, in turn, strengthens their position as strategic and technological leaders both regionally and globally. It enables them to attract international partnerships, build collaborations with renowned defence companies, and foster knowledge transfer, further spurring economic growth and diversification.

The localisation of the defence industry also has societal implications. As the GCC states progress towards self-reliance in defence production, there is a growing emphasis on developing national talent and expertise. Education and training programmes are implemented to nurture a skilled workforce capable of driving innovation, entrepreneurship, and national pride. The development of indigenous defence capabilities provides a sense of security for the population and instils a sense of national identity and self-sufficiency.

In conclusion, the localisation of the defence industry in the GCC states has fundamentally transformed power dynamics within the region and has far-reaching implications for global geopolitics. Through the growth of their defence industries, the GCC states have gained greater autonomy, reshaped alliances, and increased their influence in regional and international affairs. The rise of local defence industries can alter the balance of power among neighbouring states, disrupt traditional global defence trade patterns, and contribute to the emergence of a multipolar world order. Understanding the influence and implications of localised defence industries is crucial for comprehending the evolving dynamics of power and security in the Gulf region and its impact on a global scale. The economic, geopolitical, and societal effects of localised defence industries underscore the importance of long-term strategic planning and investment in national security and defence capabilities.

Chapter 25

Shifts in Global Geopolitics and Geo-economics

*I*n the rapidly changing global landscape, the localisation of the GCC
states' defence industry has significant implications for geopolitics and
geo-economics. As these countries strive to reduce their dependencies on external suppliers and enhance their self-reliance, they inadvertently impact
the region's power dynamics and beyond. This chapter thoroughly explores
the geopolitical and geo-economic ramifications of the GCC states' efforts to
develop their defence industries.

One of the key consequences of localisation is the potential shift in
power dynamics within the region. The GCC states traditionally rely on
external powers, particularly the United States, for their defence needs.
This has created a certain level of dependency, with external powers ex-
erting influence over regional security affairs. However, as the GCC states
increasingly develop their own defence capabilities, it could lead to a rebalancing of power and a greater degree of autonomy in decision-making.

The localisation of the defence industry has the potential to reshape
the dynamics of the Middle East. As the GCC states invest in indigenous

defence capabilities, they may seek to assert themselves as regional pow-
erhouses and enhance their influence in global affairs. This shift in power
dynamics could challenge existing global power structures and alliances,
leading to a recalibration of diplomatic relations and collaborative efforts.
The GCC states may become more assertive in shaping international security agendas and playing a more significant role in global defence trade.

Furthermore, the localisation of the defence industry can have profound
implications for regional stability. As the GCC states develop their defence
industries, a sense of self-sufficiency and resilience is created, reducing
vulnerabilities to external threats. This enhanced capacity for self-defence
can contribute to a more stable region, as the GCC states are no longer
solely reliant on external powers for their security needs. This may also
alleviate tensions and rivalries within the region as the balance of power
shifts and greater cooperation is fostered among neighbouring states.

On the geo-economic front, the localisation of the defence industry can
have profound economic consequences. By developing domestic defence
capabilities, the GCC states aim to stimulate their economies through
job creation, technological innovation, and economic diversification. The
defence industry significantly contributes to research and development,
which can lead to advancements in other sectors such as technology, manufacturing, and engineering. The potential for trickle-down technologies
and economic growth is immense, transforming these states into innovation and economic prosperity hubs.

Moreover, the localisation of the defence industry can have broader
geo-economic implications, as it may disrupt the established global defence
trade networks. The GCC states have historically been major arms importers, relying on foreign suppliers to meet their defence requirements.
However, with the development of indigenous capabilities, they can reduce their reliance on foreign arms suppliers, impacting global defence
markets. This could stimulate competition among defence companies
worldwide as they seek to capture the emerging market demand for lo-

cal defence industry development. The potential for increased trade in defence-related technologies and services also opens up new regional and international economic cooperation opportunities.

Furthermore, the localisation of the defence industry offers the GCC states enhanced strategic flexibility. By reducing their reliance on external suppliers, they can tailor their defence capabilities to suit their specific security needs and priorities. This means they can develop specialised technologies and systems that cater specifically to their unique regional challenges. This capacity for customisation bolsters their national security and allows the GCC states to cultivate knowledge-based economies with the potential for exporting defence expertise and technologies.

Additionally, the localisation of the defence industry can foster a sense of national pride and identity. As GCC states transition from importers to producers of defence equipment, it can catalyze the building of a stronger and more cohesive national defence industry. This includes investments in research and development, education and training programmes, and infrastructure development. The GCC states can develop a skilled workforce and promote innovation by nurturing a domestic defence industry, increasing national capabilities and self-sufficiency.

However, there are also challenges associated with localisation. Developing a sophisticated defence industry requires substantial investments in research and development, infrastructure, and human capital. The GCC states must overcome the technological and knowledge gaps to compete with established global players in the defence sector. This necessitates partnerships with international defence companies, technology transfers, and collaborations with leading research institutions and universities. It also demands sustained government support and a long-term strategic vision to build a sustainable and globally competitive defence industry.

In conclusion, localising the GCC states' defence industry has significant implications for global geopolitics and geo-economics. As these countries develop their domestic defence capabilities, power dynamics within the region and beyond may experience shifts, potentially challenging existing alliances and structures. It also has the potential to transform these states into centres of innovation and economic prosperity, stimulating job creation and technological advancements. Furthermore, the localisation of the defence industry may disrupt global defence trade networks, impacting foreign arms suppliers and stimulating competition in the market. These changes require careful consideration and analysis to understand their long-term effects on regional and global security dynamics. The journey towards localisation, though challenging, offers the GCC states the opportunity to shape their destiny, enhance their national capabilities, and contribute to a broader geopolitical and geo-economic transformation.

Chapter 26

Implications for Global Defence Trade

*T*he localisation of defence industries in the Gulf Cooperation Council (GCC) states has far-reaching implications for global defence trade. As these countries strive to develop their own indigenous defence capabilities, they are inevitably reducing their reliance on foreign defence imports. This trend is expected to impact various aspects of the global defence trade landscape, particularly those traditionally major exporters to the GCC region.

Firstly, the localisation efforts in the GCC states are likely to result in a decline in the volume of defence imports from traditional suppliers. As these countries develop their own defence industries, they will seek to manufacture more of their military equipment domestically. Several factors contribute to this shift in strategy.

One crucial factor is the desire for self-sufficiency and reducing dependence on foreign suppliers for critical defence capabilities. Recognising the uncertainties associated with international politics and the potential for supply disruptions, the GCC states are keen to ensure uninterrupted access to defence equipment. By establishing their own defence industries, they can reduce their vulnerability to geopolitical risks and maintain a sustained defence capability.

Another factor driving localisation is the economic diversification agenda prevalent in many GCC countries. As these nations look to reduce their reliance on oil revenues, they are actively pursuing economic diversification strategies. The defence sector presents a significant avenue for generating local employment, attracting skilled professionals, and nurturing advanced technological ecosystems. By developing their defence industries, the GCC nations can enhance their security and stimulate economic growth and innovation in other high-tech sectors.

Secondly, the increasing localisation of defence industries in the GCC may lead to greater competition in the global defence market. Historically, major defence suppliers from the United States, Europe, and Russia have dominated the market. However, with the GCC states developing their own expertise and capabilities, they may become formidable competitors to established defence manufacturers.

This potential scenario can disrupt the status quo, resulting in a more fragmented and competitive market. With their economic resources, technological ambitions, and strategic geographic location, the GCC nations can offer lucrative contracts and compete in the global defence industry. This rise in competition may lead to price pressures and encourage traditional suppliers to innovate and offer competitive advantages to retain market share.

Furthermore, the localisation of defence industries may have implications beyond the realm of production and trade. It can foster national pride, enhance regional security cooperation, and stimulate research and development. Establishing indigenous defence capabilities allows the GCC states to demonstrate their sovereignty and ability to defend their territories. It also creates opportunities for collaboration and knowledge sharing within the region, leading to a more integrated and self-reliant defence ecosystem.

Thirdly, localising defence industries may facilitate technology transfer and knowledge sharing between the GCC states and their global defence partners. The GCC nations have actively pursued collaborations with established defence manufacturers, recognising the necessity of acquiring advanced technologies. These collaborations enable the transfer of specialised technological know-how, manufacturing techniques, and research and development capabilities.

Such knowledge exchange plays a crucial role in the growth of the GCC defence industries. It allows them to leverage the expertise of established defence suppliers while simultaneously developing their own indigenous capabilities. This symbiotic relationship fosters interdependence between the GCC states and their global defence partners, creating a more interconnected global defence ecosystem.

Moreover, the localisation of defence industries may also result in the emergence of new export opportunities for the GCC defence manufacturers. As these countries develop innovative defence technologies and capabilities, they seek avenues to export their products to international markets. Expanding export capabilities can potentially disrupt the existing global defence trade dynamics.

Armed with competitive products and lower production costs, GCC defence manufacturers can offer attractive alternatives to established suppliers. This could lead to a reshuffling of market share and force traditional suppliers to reassess their strategies. Consequently, the emergence of new players in the defence manufacturing sector may increase the diversity of defence offerings in the global marketplace.

Furthermore, the localisation of defence industries in the GCC states may have implications for alliances and geopolitical relationships. As these nations become more self-reliant in their defence production, they may become less dependent on traditional suppliers. This has the potential to impact diplomatic and strategic ties.

GCC states could establish new alliances and partnerships with countries offering advanced defence technologies or collaborative opportunities. These partnerships may extend beyond manufacturing and incorporate joint research and development, intelligence sharing, and joint military exercises. The evolving dynamics in the GCC defence sector may influence geopolitical landscapes as nations adapt to the changing realities and opportunities in the industry.

In conclusion, localising defence industries in the GCC states has significant implications for global defence trade. The decline in defence imports, increased competition, technology transfer, emergence of new export opportunities, and potential shifts in defence alliances all shape the global defence trade landscape.

Traditional defence suppliers need to adapt their strategies and offerings to remain competitive in the evolving marketplace. At the same time, the localisation efforts in the GCC serve as an opportunity for collaboration, knowledge sharing, and the establishment of new partnerships. Ultimately, the interconnectedness of global defence trade will continue to evolve as the GCC states further develop their indigenous defence capabilities.

Chapter 27

Security Implications of Localised Defence Industries

Integration of AI and Advanced Technologies

I n this era of rapid technological advancements, the localisation of
defence industries in the Gulf Cooperation Council (GCC) states
has deep-rooted security implications. Integrating artificial intelligence
(AI) and advanced technologies into the defence sector brings profound
changes and poses opportunities and challenges. By adopting AI-enabled
systems, such as unmanned aerial vehicles (UAVs), autonomous vehicles,
and robotic platforms, GCC states can enhance their military capabilities
to unprecedented levels.

AI systems can revolutionise surveillance and reconnaissance by providing real-time intelligence and enhancing situational awareness on the
battlefield. UAVs equipped with AI algorithms can autonomously identify
and track targets, gather valuable data, and conduct precise strikes, thus
reducing human error and response time. Moreover, integrating AI in
decision-making processes through machine learning algorithms can aid

in analysing complex data sets and optimising military operations. This technology can assist military commanders in formulating strategies and predicting potential security threats, ultimately leading to more efficient resource allocation and operational success.

Additionally, integrating advanced technologies, such as virtual reality (VR) and augmented reality (AR), into training programmes allows for realistic simulations of combat scenarios and enhances the skillsets of military personnel. Through immersive training experiences, soldiers can acquire practical knowledge and refine their tactical abilities, leading to increased effectiveness in real-world missions.

Defence Doctrines and Strategies in Cybersecurity, Hybrid Warfare, and Maritime Security

The localisation of defence industries empowers GCC states to develop and adapt defence doctrines and strategies that precisely address contemporary security challenges. In the realm of cybersecurity, localisation enables the implementation of holistic approaches to safeguard critical military and civilian infrastructure against cyber threats. Through the establishment of indigenous capabilities in cybersecurity, GCC states can develop robust encryption methods, intrusion detection systems, and threat intelligence sharing mechanisms. Furthermore, a domestic cybersecurity industry will drive research and development in cutting-edge technologies, contributing to international cybersecurity advancements.

As hybrid warfare emerges as a prominent threat, the localisation of defence industries allows GCC states to develop comprehensive defensive capabilities. This entails integrating traditional military strategies with unconventional tactics, such as cyber-attacks, disinformation campaigns, and proxy warfare. By focusing on developing countermeasures against hybrid warfare, GCC states can enhance their ability to neutralise threats and protect their sovereign interests from external adversaries.

Furthermore, the localisation of defence industries enables the development of advanced maritime security strategies. Given the strategic coastal locations and reliance on maritime trade routes, the GCC states place immense importance on securing their maritime borders. Localisation facilitates the development of maritime domain awareness systems that encompass radar systems, sonar systems, and coastal surveillance platforms. These capabilities ensure the protection of maritime sovereignty, the security of vital trade routes, and the ability to swiftly respond to potential security threats, including piracy, smuggling, and unauthorised maritime intrusions.

Strengthening GCC States' Armed Forces

The localisation of defence industries plays a vital role in bolstering the armed forces of GCC states. By reducing reliance on external suppliers, GCC states gain greater autonomy and control over their military capabilities, ensuring operations continuity even in geopolitical uncertainties. The establishment of indigenous defence industries fosters a sense of self-sufficiency and resilience, allowing states to respond swiftly and effectively to emerging security threats.

Additionally, localisation enables the customisation and adaptation of defence equipment based on regional challenges and requirements. GCC states can incorporate specific operational needs, geographical factors, and climatic considerations into developing and producing advanced military systems. This tailored approach ensures that defence capabilities are optimised for the unique security landscape of the region.

Moreover, localisation promotes collaboration and partnership between GCC states in defence research, development, and production. By pooling resources and expertise, states can leverage each other's strengths and achieve technological advancements that benefit the entire region. Collaborative projects allow for knowledge sharing, joint training exercises, and interoperability, enhancing the collective security of the GCC states.

Furthermore, the localisation of defence industries promotes economic diversification and creates job opportunities within the GCC states. The growth of defence industries encourages the development of a skilled workforce and provides technological know-how, allowing knowledge transfer and indigenous innovation to thrive. This, in turn, enhances the overall socio-economic development of the region.

In conclusion, localising defence industries in the GCC states has profound security implications. Integrating AI and advanced technologies enhances military capabilities, enabling real-time situational awareness, efficient decision-making, and realistic training experiences. Through the development of tailored defence doctrines and strategies, GCC states address contemporary security challenges, including cybersecurity, hybrid warfare, and maritime security. Moreover, localisation strengthens the armed forces by reducing external dependencies, promoting collaboration, and enhancing operational effectiveness. The economic benefits of defence industries further contribute to the region's overall security, stability, and prosperity.

Chapter 28

Integration of AI and Advanced Technologies

*I*n recent years, the Gulf Cooperation Council (GCC) states have recognised the increasingly crucial role of advanced technologies, particularly artificial intelligence (AI), in enhancing their defence capabilities. This
chapter explores the integration of AI and other advanced technologies in the
GCC states' defence industries and its implications for regional security.

1. Leveraging AI in Defence:

Artificial Intelligence (AI) is an umbrella term encompassing various
technologies and techniques that simulate, replicate, or mimic human
cognitive abilities. It includes machine learning, computer vision, natural
language processing, and robotics. The GCC states have embraced AI
to enhance their defence capabilities, allowing for state-of-the-art military
operations.

a. Definition and Components of AI:

Artificial Intelligence refers to the ability of machines to perform tasks that usually require human intelligence. It involves computer systems learning from data, recognising patterns, making decisions, and solving complex problems through algorithms. It comprises perception, reasoning, and action, key components for effective military applications.

b. Application of AI in Military Operations:

AI has revolutionised military operations, introducing sophisticated systems to augment and automate various tasks, reducing human involvement and increasing efficiency. Examples include autonomous systems for surveillance, target tracking, and decision-making processes. It empowers the military to overcome operational limitations and respond rapidly to evolving security challenges.

c. Use of AI in Intelligence Analysis and Decision Making:

AI has enabled significant advancements in intelligence analysis and decision-making processes. Machine learning algorithms can process vast amounts of data from multiple sources, analyse patterns, and swiftly identify potential risks or threats. This capability enhances situational awareness, enabling timely and informed decision-making for defence personnel.

2. Advancements in Robotics and Autonomous Systems:

The progress of AI has gone hand in hand with advancements in robotics and autonomous systems, introducing unmanned platforms that can perform a range of military functions.

a. Development of Unmanned Aerial Vehicles (UAVs):

UAVs, commonly known as drones, have become integral to defence operations. These unmanned aircraft can be deployed for intelligence gathering, surveillance, reconnaissance, and targeted strikes. With AI, UAVs can autonomously navigate complex environments, adapt to changing situations, and execute missions efficiently.

b. Autonomous Ground Vehicles and Robotics:

Ground vehicles equipped with AI and robotics have diversified military capabilities. Autonomous ground vehicles can be deployed for logistical support, patrolling, and even combat operations. Robots with AI algorithms can operate in hazardous environments, assist in demining operations, and provide medical support on the battlefield.

c. Use of Drones for Surveillance and Targeting:

AI-driven drones have become pivotal for surveillance and targeting in modern warfare. These unmanned systems are equipped with advanced sensors and AI algorithms, enabling accurate target identification, tracking, and engagement. They facilitate precise strikes while minimising collateral damage and reducing risks to human personnel.

3. Cybersecurity and AI:

As the integration of advanced technology grows, the GCC states recognise the need to bolster their cybersecurity defences. AI can play a significant role in fortifying cybersecurity measures, providing proactive protection against emerging cyber threats.

a. Role of AI in Enhancing Cyber Defence:
AI can assist in analysing vast amounts of data to identify patterns and anomalies, detect cyber threats, and formulate proactive countermeasures. Machine learning algorithms can continuously learn from real-time data, enabling organisations to defend against evolving cyber threats effectively.

b. Detecting and Responding to Cyber Threats:
AI-based cyber defence systems can autonomously detect and respond to cyber threats in real time. These systems can swiftly identify and neutralise potential cyber-attacks by analysing network traffic, monitoring abnormal behaviour, and deploying automated response mechanisms.

c. Challenges and Opportunities in Cybersecurity:
While AI holds great promise for cybersecurity, challenges persist. Adversarial attacks on AI systems can deceive or compromise their functionality. Continuous updates and improvements are necessary to stay ahead of sophisticated threats. Moreover, there is a need to balance privacy concerns with AI-powered cybersecurity measures to protect sensitive data.

4. AI and Information Warfare:

The integration of AI in defence strategies has expanded the realm of information warfare, enabling more effective information gathering, analysis, and dissemination.

a. Utilising AI in Information Gathering and Analysis:
AI helps military intelligence agencies sift through vast amounts of

data, including open-source information, social media, and satellite imagery. Machine learning algorithms can identify patterns, extract relevant information, and provide valuable insights to support decision-making processes.

b. Influence Operations and Psychological Warfare:
AI-powered systems enable improved influence operations and psychological warfare. By analysing vast amounts of online information, AI algorithms can identify target demographics, tailor messages, and shape narratives to influence public opinion.

c. Counteracting Disinformation and Fake News:
AI can also play a crucial role in combating disinformation and fake news. With automated detection systems, AI algorithms can identify misleading or false information, track its spread, and inform decision-makers to counteract its impact on public perception and national security.

5. Challenges in Integrating AI in Defence:

While AI integration in defence brings numerous advantages, several challenges must be considered for its effective implementation.

a. Ethical and Legal Concerns:
The use of AI in defence raises ethical questions surrounding its deployment in autonomous weapons and decision-making. Ensuring transparency, adherence to international laws and regulations, and accountability are central to addressing these concerns.

b. Maintaining Data Security and Privacy:
AI relies on vast amounts of data, creating the potential for breaches, insider threats, or unauthorised access. Securing data and protecting individual privacy are crucial considerations when integrating AI in defence

systems.

c. Developing a Skilled Workforce in AI:
The successful integration of AI in defence requires a skilled workforce capable of developing, operating, and maintaining these systems. Promoting AI education, training programmes, and collaboration with academic institutions are essential to bridge the skills gap in the defence industry.

6. Collaboration and Partnerships:

Collaborative efforts and partnerships play a vital role in AI integration in defence, offering opportunities for knowledge exchange and joint research and development.

a. International Cooperation in AI and Defence:
The GCC states can benefit from international collaboration in AI research, innovation, and defence capabilities. Partnering with technologically advanced countries and institutions can facilitate the adoption of best practices, sharing expertise, and joint investments in AI development.

b. Opportunities for Knowledge Exchange and Collaboration:
Organising workshops, conferences, and joint exercises can foster fruitful exchanges and collaboration among GCC member states and external partners. These engagements enable sharing experiences, lessons learnt, and innovative approaches to AI integration in defence.

c. Potential for Joint Research and Development:
Collaborative research in AI and defence among GCC states can yield significant advancements. Sharing resources, expertise, and infrastructure can streamline technological development, reduce redundancies, and accelerate the deployment of cutting-edge AI systems.

7. Implications of Military Strategies:

Integrating AI in defence strategies necessitates reevaluating military doctrines, structures, and operational methodologies.

a. Shifts in Warfare Paradigms and Doctrines:

AI-powered technologies are causing shifts in warfare paradigms, transforming doctrines and conventional operational tactics. Military strategies need to adapt to effectively leverage the advantages offered by AI to maintain a competitive edge on the modern battlefield.

b. Balancing Human Decision-Making with AI Assistance:

While AI systems can enhance decision-making processes, human judgment remains indispensable. Striking the right balance between human expertise and AI assistance is crucial to ensure AI's responsible and ethical use in defence. Humans must ultimately retain control over AI systems and be able to exercise judgement and discretion in critical decision-making processes.

c. Enhanced Situational Awareness and Rapid Decision-Making:

AI systems can provide real-time, accurate, and comprehensive situational awareness, enabling defence personnel to make informed decisions swiftly. Integrating AI in defence can reduce response times, enhance operational effectiveness, and increase mission success rates.

d. Increased Efficiency and Resource Optimisation:

AI integration in defence can optimise resource allocation and utilisation. By automating routine tasks and streamlining operations, AI enables defence organisations to allocate their resources more efficiently, allowing for better utilisation of manpower and assets.

e. A Paradigm Shift in Defence Industries:

Integrating AI in defence industries demands a paradigm shift in defence organisations' operations. Traditional defence industries must embrace AI as a core component of their operations, investing in research and development, acquiring AI capabilities, and developing a workforce with AI skills.

f. Implications for Regional Security:

Integrating AI and advanced technologies in defence industries has significant implications for regional security in the Gulf Cooperation Council region. AI-powered military capabilities can enhance deterrence, reduce vulnerabilities, and strengthen defence capabilities. However, regional actors' widespread adoption of AI may also lead to an arms race, potentially escalating tensions and undermining regional stability.

Conclusion:

The integration of AI and advanced technologies in defence industries of the Gulf Cooperation Council states presents significant opportunities and challenges. AI can revolutionise military operations, enhance intelligence analysis, fortify cybersecurity defences, and reshape information warfare. However, AI's responsible and ethical implementation requires careful consideration of legal, ethical, and privacy concerns. Collaboration, partnerships, and investment in AI research and development are key to maximising the benefits of AI integration in defence and ensuring regional security in the GCC states.

Chapter 29

Defense Doctrines and Strategies in Cybersecurity, Hybrid Warfare, and Maritime Security

*I*n an increasingly interconnected world, the defence doctrines and strategies of Gulf Cooperation Council (GCC) states have evolved to address emerging challenges in cybersecurity, hybrid warfare, and maritime security. This chapter provides an in-depth exploration of the various aspects of these defence domains and their implications for the GCC countries.

1. Cybersecurity:

Rapid technological advancements have brought about an unprecedented reliance on cyberspace for communication, commerce, and critical infrastructure. GCC states have acknowledged cybersecurity's importance and developed comprehensive doctrines to safeguard their networks, systems, and information.

a. Cyber Threat Landscape:

The GCC region faces a diverse and evolving cyber threat landscape, requiring constant adaptation to stay ahead of potential risks. State-sponsored attacks pose significant challenges, with intelligence agencies from
various countries targeting GCC states for political and economic espionage. These attacks often manifest in the form of sophisticated malware,
phishing campaigns, and targeted social engineering.

Non-state actors, such as hacktivists and cybercriminals, also pose considerable threats by aiming to disrupt services, steal sensitive data, or engage
in cyber espionage for financial gain. Cybersecurity is further complicated by the emergence of advanced persistent threats (APTs) that conduct
long-term cyber espionage activities, usually attributed to state-sponsored
actors.

b. Defensive Measures:

GCC states have taken a multi-faceted approach to strengthen their cybersecurity defences. They have established dedicated Computer Emergency
Response Teams (CERTs) to respond promptly to cyber incidents and coordinate efforts to mitigate risks. These CERTs are responsible for incident
response, vulnerability management, and providing guidance and support
to government agencies, critical infrastructure, and private sector entities.

Robust legal frameworks and cybercrime laws have been enacted to
address cyber offences and facilitate cooperation between law enforcement
agencies and cybersecurity entities. These legal measures serve as a deterrent and enable the prosecution of cybercriminals and malicious actors.

Significant investments in cutting-edge cybersecurity technologies, including intrusion detection systems, encryption tools, and advanced firewalls, have been made by GCC states. They employ a defence-in-depth approach, combining technological solutions with comprehensive training programmes for cybersecurity personnel. These initiatives aim to build a skilled workforce capable of effectively detecting and responding to cyber threats.

Furthermore, GCC states recognise the importance of cross-border collaboration and information sharing in enhancing their cybersecurity defences. Initiatives such as the Arab Regional Cyber Security Centre (ARCC), a collaborative effort supported by Gulf states, facilitate sharing of threat intelligence and best practices among member countries. These partnerships help identify emerging threats, enhance incident response capabilities, and foster a collective defence approach against cyber threats.

c. Cyber Warfare Capabilities:

Recognising the potential impact of offensive cyber operations, GCC states have developed their offensive and defensive cyber warfare capabilities to deter potential threats and respond effectively. They aim to defend their networks, critical infrastructure, and national interests by establishing cyber forces within their armed forces. These forces focus on developing intelligence-gathering capabilities, disrupting adversaries' networks, and conducting retaliatory cyber operations as deemed necessary.

GCC states invest in advanced research and development programmes to further enhance their cyber warfare capabilities. These efforts include staying updated with emerging technologies such as artificial intelligence, quantum computing, and blockchain and developing cybersecurity solutions tailored to their specific needs.

2. Hybrid Warfare:

Hybrid warfare refers to blending conventional and unconventional military tactics, including information warfare, economic coercion, proxy forces, and cyberattacks. GCC states recognise the need to counter these hybrid threats and have adjusted their doctrines and strategies accordingly.

a. Hybrid Threat Landscape:

The Gulf region is particularly vulnerable to hybrid threats due to its geostrategic significance and ongoing conflicts. Various state and non-state actors use tactics to further their interests, creating complex security challenges. Destabilisation efforts, support for proxy groups, disinformation campaigns, economic coercion, and cyberattacks are among the tactics that hybrid warfare encompasses.

Key actors engaging in hybrid warfare in the Gulf region include state-sponsored organisations, terrorist groups, proxy networks, and non-state actors seeking to undermine security and stability.

b. Countermeasures:

GCC states have implemented a range of countermeasures to address hybrid threats effectively. Close cooperation and intelligence sharing among GCC states and international partners are crucial in identifying and countering destabilising activities, ensuring rapid responses to emerging threats.

Enhancing border security through advanced surveillance technologies, increased patrols, and coordination among relevant agencies helps prevent infiltration and smuggling of arms, drugs, or illicit goods. GCC states also invest in capacity building in neighbouring countries to enhance their resilience against hybrid threats, fostering regional stability.

In countering disinformation and information warfare, GCC states focus on building resilient societies to withstand manipulative campaigns. This involves promoting media literacy, countering false narratives, strengthening social cohesion, and fostering national unity. Public awareness campaigns, educational programmes, and the development of analytical capabilities to detect and expose disinformation are key elements of their strategy.

GCC states also reinforce cybersecurity measures to protect critical infrastructure and counter cyber hybrid threats. This includes conducting vulnerability assessments, implementing incident response plans, and increasing cooperation with international partners to ensure a coordinated approach to cyber defence.

c. Role of Proxy Forces:

Proxy forces play a significant role in hybrid warfare, often deployed by external actors to further their interests in the Gulf region. GCC states understand the importance of effectively managing and neutralising proxy actors to safeguard their security and national interests. Efforts include diplomatic engagements, intelligence sharing, and, if necessary, military operations to disrupt and expose the actions of proxy forces.

By unmasking external support and highlighting the consequences of proxy activities, GCC states actively work towards eroding the influence of proxy networks and encouraging sustainable stability in the region.

3. Maritime Security:

The Gulf region's critical importance as a major global energy hub and trade route makes maritime security a top priority for GCC states. Ensuring maritime traffic safety, protecting offshore resources, and countering threats from piracy, terrorism, smuggling, territorial disputes, illegal fishing, and environmental risks are paramount concerns.

a. Maritime Threats:

Maritime threats in the Gulf region are multifaceted and constantly evolving. Piracy remains a significant concern, with historical hotspots, such as the Gulf of Aden and the Arabian Sea, posing risks to international shipping. Terrorist organisations seek to exploit maritime routes for illicit activities and target maritime infrastructure to disrupt regional stability.

Smuggling, including arms trafficking, narcotics, and human smuggling, continues to challenge security efforts in the Gulf region. In addition, territorial disputes, particularly in the Arabian Gulf, can escalate tensions and trigger potential maritime conflicts. Illegal, unreported, and unregulated (IUU) fishing also threatens the sustainability of marine resources, affecting both economic and environmental aspects of maritime security.

b. Maritime Defence Strategies:

GCC states have implemented various defence strategies to address maritime security threats effectively. Strengthening naval capabilities and fostering collaboration among regional navies is crucial to ensure a strong deterrence against potential threats.

Maritime patrols and surveillance operations in territorial waters and exclusive economic zones (EEZs) are vital for surveillance, detection, and interception of potential threats. These operations encompass a combination of surface assets, naval vessels, and aerial platforms to monitor activities and respond swiftly to any security incidents.

Enhanced intelligence sharing, interoperability, and joint exercises among GCC states and international partners contribute to maritime security. Cooperation with international naval forces, such as Combined Maritime Forces (CMF) and Maritime Security Centre - Horn of Africa (MSCHOA), helps strengthen maritime security efforts and enables effective response to piracy and other maritime threats.

To combat smuggling and trade in illicit goods, GCC states collaborate with international organisations, such as the United Nations Office on Drugs and Crime (UNODC), and implement comprehensive port security measures. These measures include using advanced technologies for cargo scanning, strict customs controls, and interagency coordination to detect and apprehend smugglers.

Efforts to address territorial disputes and ensure stability in the Arabian Gulf involve diplomatic negotiations, dialogues, and confidence-building measures. GCC states actively engage in regional forums, such as the Gulf Cooperation Council and the Arab League, to promote peaceful resolutions to maritime boundary disputes and avoid conflicts.

Furthermore, GCC states recognise the importance of addressing environmental risks and promoting sustainable maritime practices. They cooperate with international bodies, like the International Maritime Organisation (IMO), to enforce regulations and implement measures to prevent pollution, mitigate the impacts of climate change, and protect marine ecosystems.

In conclusion, GCC states' defence doctrines and strategies have evolved to address emerging challenges in cybersecurity, hybrid warfare, and maritime security. The reliance on cyberspace, the evolving nature of hybrid threats, and the critical importance of maritime security have driven GCC states to develop comprehensive approaches to safeguard their interests and enhance regional stability. GCC states strive to deter potential adversaries, protect critical infrastructure, and ensure the region's stability through investment in cybersecurity, develop offensive and defensive cyber warfare capabilities, cooperate in countering hybrid threats, and strengthen maritime security measures.

Chapter 30

Strengthening GCC State's Armed Forces

*T**he chapter focuses on the various measures and strategies that can be adopted to strengthen the armed forces of the Gulf Cooperation Council (GCC) states. By enhancing the capabilities and readiness of their armed forces, the GCC states can effectively address regional security challenges and protect their national interests. This chapter explores key areas for improvement and examines potential solutions to bolster the strength of these armed forces.*

1. Enhancing Training and Exercises:

1.1 Continuous Training: Developing a highly skilled and capable military workforce is crucial for the strength of the GCC armed forces. Regular training programmes should be conducted to maintain soldiers' combat readiness, incorporating physical fitness, marksmanship, small unit tactics, and leadership development. Specialised training should also focus on counterterrorism, asymmetric warfare, and urban warfare to effectively respond to evolving threats. Moreover, training should include cultural sensitivity and language skills to ensure effective communication and collaboration with local communities during peacekeeping operations.

1.2 Joint Exercises: Joint exercises among GCC states and international partners should be conducted regularly to promote interoperability and enhance collective defence capabilities. These exercises should simulate realistic scenarios and cover various operations, including amphibious assaults, air defence exercises, and counterinsurgency scenarios. Joint exercises allow one to test command and control systems, develop cooperation, and improve tactical coordination. It is crucial to involve all branches of the armed forces in these joint exercises to enhance their ability to work together seamlessly.

1.3 Simulation Programmes: Utilising cutting-edge simulation technologies can significantly enhance training effectiveness and reduce costs. Simulators can replicate various combat scenarios, from land operations to air and naval engagements, allowing soldiers to practise in a realistic and safe environment. These programmes can also simulate operating in challenging environments such as deserts, mountains, or urban areas, providing valuable experience to the armed forces. Additionally, virtual reality (VR) and augmented reality (AR) technologies can be integrated into training programmes to enhance situational awareness, decision-making, and battlefield visualisation.

2. Modernising Defence Equipment and Technologies:

2.1 Defence Procurement: The continuous modernisation of defence equipment is essential to ensure that the GCC armed forces remain technologically advanced and effective. Robust defence procurement processes should be established to identify and acquire the most advanced weaponry, including fighter jets, main battle tanks, armoured vehicles, and missile defence systems. The procurement process should prioritise efficiency, transparency, and the selection of systems that address specific regional

challenges. Indigenous defence industry capabilities must also be emphasised to reduce dependence on foreign suppliers and foster technological
self-reliance.

2.2 Research and Development: GCC states should invest in research
and development (R&D) to foster innovation and stimulate the domestic
defence industry. Partnerships between defence organisations and research
institutes can provide opportunities to develop indigenous defence technologies while providing avenues for knowledge transfer and skill development. Encouraging collaboration with international defence industries
and academia can further enhance R&D capabilities. Emphasis should
be placed on emerging fields such as unmanned systems, directed energy
weapons, hypersonic technologies, and artificial intelligence to stay ahead
in the technological race.

2.3 Emerging Technologies: Embracing emerging technologies can provide a competitive edge in modern warfare. GCC states should explore
the integration of artificial intelligence, robotics, drones, and unmanned
systems into their armed forces. These emerging technologies can be employed for reconnaissance, surveillance, logistics, and even combat operations, reducing personnel risks while increasing operational effectiveness.
Autonomous systems, such as unmanned ground vehicles and unmanned
aerial vehicles, can be deployed for hazardous or time-sensitive tasks, freeing up human resources for higher-level decision-making and critical operations.

3. Improving Intelligence, Surveillance, and Reconnais-
sance (ISR) Capabilities:

3.1 Advanced ISR Systems: The GCC armed forces should invest in
advanced ISR capabilities to strengthen situational awareness and intelligence-gathering capabilities. Satellite systems, airborne surveillance plat-

forms, and unmanned aerial vehicles should be acquired or developed to provide real-time intelligence on potential threats, monitor critical infrastructure, and facilitate rapid response. Integrating advanced sensor technologies, including radar systems, electro-optical sensors, and synthetic aperture radar (SAR), can enhance surveillance capabilities, especially in challenging weather or terrain conditions.

3.2 Intelligence Networks: Collaboration and information sharing among GCC states are vital for effective intelligence gathering. The establishment of robust intelligence networks that facilitate the exchange of information, including human intelligence (HUMINT), signals intelligence (SIGINT), and open-source intelligence (OSINT), can provide timely and accurate assessments. Sharing resources, expertise, and intelligence assets can significantly enhance the intelligence capabilities of each GCC state. This collaboration should also extend to international intelligence partnerships, promoting cooperation in intelligence analysis and counterterrorism efforts.

3.3 Cyber Intelligence: With the increasing importance of cyber domains, developing robust cyber intelligence capabilities is essential. GCC states should invest in cyber defence units that monitor, analyse, and counter cyber threats. Advanced monitoring tools, threat intelligence sharing platforms, and partnerships with international cybersecurity agencies can strengthen cyber intelligence capabilities, allowing for proactive defence against cyber-attacks. Cybersecurity awareness and training should also be integrated into the armed forces' educational programmes to ensure a cyber-resilient workforce.

4. Enhancing Maritime Security:

4.1 Naval Acquisition: Given their geographically strategic position, GCC states need to enhance their naval capabilities. Acquiring modern naval vessels, including frigates, corvettes, submarines, and patrol boats, should be prioritised to ensure maritime dominance. These vessels should have advanced sensor systems, anti-ship missiles, and anti-submarine warfare capabilities to safeguard territorial waters and regional maritime trade routes. In addition to conventional naval forces, developing naval special forces units capable of conducting maritime counterterrorism operations and engaging in asymmetric warfare is crucial.

4.2 Maritime Surveillance Systems: Comprehensive maritime surveillance systems, such as coastal radars, marine AIS (Automatic Identification System), and underwater sonar systems, are vital for effective maritime domain awareness. GCC states should invest in these systems to detect and track potential threats, monitor vessel movements, enforce maritime regulations, and deter piracy. Furthermore, integrating unmanned maritime systems, such as autonomous surface vessels and underwater drones, can augment surveillance capabilities, especially in vast and remote maritime areas.

4.3 International Cooperation: Close cooperation with regional and international partners is crucial for ensuring maritime security. GCC states should actively engage in joint patrols, intelligence sharing, and capacity-building programmes to combat piracy, smuggling, and other maritime threats. Sharing best practices, conducting joint maritime exercises, and fostering regional maritime cooperation will strengthen the collective security of the GCC states. Additionally, participating in multinational naval task forces, such as Combined Maritime Forces (CMF) and counter-piracy operations, can contribute to maintaining a secure maritime environment in the region.

5. Cybersecurity and Information Warfare:

5.1 Robust Cybersecurity Measures: As reliance on information technology grows, the GCC armed forces must invest in robust cybersecurity measures to protect against cyber threats. Developing advanced cybersecurity frameworks, implementing encryption technology, and adopting secure data storage practices are essential. Creating specialised cyber defence units capable of detecting, responding to, and mitigating cyber-attacks is also critical. Regular auditing of systems, vulnerability assessments, and penetration testing should be conducted to identify and rectify potential weaknesses in the cybersecurity infrastructure.

5.2 Offensive and Defensive Cyber Capabilities: GCC states should develop offensive and defensive cyber capabilities to deter and respond to cyber-attacks. Offensive cyber capabilities can disrupt or disable enemy networks and systems, while defensive capabilities focus on protecting critical infrastructure and networks from cyber threats. Developing skilled cyber personnel, establishing cyber response teams, and conducting regular cyber exercises will enhance the effectiveness of these capabilities.

5.3 Information Warfare: Information warfare has become critical to modern conflicts. GCC armed forces should develop strategies and capabilities to engage in information warfare, including psychological operations, propaganda dissemination, and influence campaigns. This involves leveraging social media, news outlets, and other communication channels to shape public opinion, counter misinformation, and project a positive narrative. Cooperation with international partners experienced in information warfare can provide valuable insights and resources.

6. Strengthening Special Operations Forces (SOF):

6.1 Specialised Training: Special Operations Forces (SOF) play a crucial role in counterterrorism operations, unconventional warfare, and special reconnaissance. Appropriate and specialised training should be provided to enhance the capabilities of these forces. This includes advanced marksmanship, combat diving, airborne operations, and hostage rescue training. Language proficiency, cultural awareness, and intelligence-gathering skills are essential for successful SOF operations. Regular joint training exercises with international SOF units will promote interoperability and best practice exchange.

6.2 Specialised Equipment: Equipping SOF units with state-of-the-art gear and specialised equipment is crucial. This includes advanced communications systems, night vision devices, lightweight body armour, and specialised weapons. Using unmanned systems, such as drones and unmanned ground vehicles, can also enhance the capabilities of SOF units, enabling them to gather intelligence and conduct covert operations in high-risk areas.

6.3 Integration and Coordination: Special Operations Forces should be integrated into the overall military structure and coordination mechanisms. Close collaboration with conventional forces, intelligence, and law enforcement agencies is essential for effective mission planning and execution. Establishing joint operations centres and developing interoperable command and control systems will enable seamless coordination and information sharing.

7. Enhancing Defence Industrial Capacity:

7.1 Indigenous Defence Industry: GCC states should prioritise the development of their domestic defence industries to reduce dependence on foreign suppliers and foster technological self-reliance. This requires investment in research and development, establishing defence technology parks, and promoting collaboration between the defence industry and research institutes. Encouraging joint ventures and partnerships with international defence companies can also facilitate technology transfer and knowledge sharing.

7.2 Defence Exports: Developing a competitive defence industry can also open avenues for defence exports, generating revenue and enhancing the reputation of GCC states in the global defence market. GCC states should focus on producing high-quality defence equipment and technology that caters to the requirements of regional and international customers. Exporting defence products can also strengthen diplomatic and strategic relationships with partner countries.

7.3 Skilled Workforce: Developing a skilled workforce is vital for the success of the defence industry. GCC states should invest in educational programs focusing on science, technology, engineering, and mathematics (STEM) fields, crucial for defence industry innovation. Collaborations with international defence companies and educational institutions can provide skills development and knowledge transfer opportunities.

In conclusion, strengthening the armed forces of GCC states requires comprehensive measures and strategies. These include enhancing training and exercises, modernising defence equipment and technologies, improving intelligence, surveillance, and reconnaissance capabilities, enhancing maritime security, investing in cybersecurity and information warfare capabilities, strengthening special operations forces, and developing a robust defence industrial capacity. By focusing on these areas, GCC states can effectively address regional security challenges and protect their national interests.

Chapter 31

Diplomatic Relations and Collaborations

In this chapter, we will explore the effects of the localisation of the defence industry in the Gulf Cooperation Council (GCC) states on diplomatic relationships and collaborations. The move towards the indigenisation of the defence industry has significant implications for both regional and international diplomacy. This requires a thorough reassessment of current alliances, dependencies, and geopolitical dynamics.

One significant aspect to consider is redefining diplomatic alliances in the region. As the GCC states develop their own defence capabilities, they may no longer rely as heavily on external military support. This could shift the balance of power in the region and lead to new diplomatic partnerships. The emergence of the GCC states as self-sufficient defence actors may compel other nations to recalibrate their diplomatic strategies, prompting the potential realignment of alliances. This dynamic, in turn, could impact regional stability and influence global power dynamics.

The localisation of the defence industry also has profound implications for global diplomacy. As the GCC states decrease their dependence on arms imports and establish their own defence manufacturing capabilities, they become substantial players in the global defence market. This newfound economic and technological prowess opens up possibilities for increased collaborations with other countries in defence technology transfers and joint defence projects. The GCC states' emergence as defence industry leaders could contribute to a more cooperative and synergistic international security landscape.

Furthermore, developing local defence industries fosters avenues for enhanced regional cooperation. As neighbouring countries in the Gulf region pursue similar goals of indigenisation, there is potential for collaboration in research, development, and production of defence technologies. This could lead to the formation of closer bonds between nations, promoting regional security and stability. Collaborative initiatives, such as joint military exercises, intelligence sharing, and coordinated responses to common security challenges, could mitigate conflicts and promote a sense of collective security within the GCC and its neighbouring countries.

Moreover, localising the defence industry in the GCC states brings economic and technological benefits that can enhance diplomatic relations and collaborations. The growth of indigenous defence industries stimulates job creation, innovation, and technology transfer, attracting global investments and fostering knowledge sharing. This strengthens the GCC states' domestic capabilities and establishes them as attractive partners for international collaboration. By engaging in joint research and development programmes with international partners, the GCC states can harness the expertise and resources of established defence industries to enhance their own capabilities further.

However, the localisation of the defence industry may also strain diplomatic relations, particularly with traditional arms suppliers. As the GCC states reduce their reliance on imports, countries that have historically been major arms providers may perceive the emerging local defence industries as competition. This situation adds complexity to managing diplomatic ties, as the GCC states must balance their desire for self-reliance in defence with maintaining healthy relationships with their traditional allies. Navigating these potentially tense diplomatic dynamics requires careful analysis, adept negotiation, and strategic decision-making.

Furthermore, localising the defence industry in the GCC states could have wider implications for global security dynamics. The emergence of new defence players in the region may alter the perception of the Gulf as a critical strategic hub, attracting attention and engagement from global powers. Regional and international actors might seek to establish or strengthen partnerships with the GCC states to seize economic opportunities, secure access to energy resources, or maintain influence over regional security affairs. However, these interactions can also generate complex power dynamics and unintended consequences.

Moreover, the localisation of the defence industry can lead to the development of indigenous defence technologies with broader market potential. As the GCC states invest in research and development, they may produce cutting-edge defence systems and technologies that are relevant to their own defence needs and global customers. This opens up opportunities for export-oriented collaborations, joint ventures, and technology transfers, thereby expanding the scope of diplomatic relations and fostering economic integration.

In conclusion, localising the defence industry in the GCC states brings about substantial diplomatic ramifications. It necessitates reevaluating existing alliances, fostering new collaborations, managing potential tensions, and adapting to evolving geopolitical dynamics. As the GCC states assert their independence in the defence sector, their diplomatic relations undergo a transformative phase, with implications for both regional and global politics. The interconnectedness of diplomacy and defence industry localisation calls for careful analysis, open dialogue, and proactive strategies from policymakers and defence officials to maximise opportunities for stability, cooperation, and shared security in the evolving landscape of the Gulf region.

Chapter 32

Redefining Diplomatic Alliances and Dependencies

*I*n this chapter, we will explore the effects of the localisation of the defence industry in the Gulf Cooperation Council (GCC) countries on diplomatic relations and collaborations. By localising their defence industry, GCC countries can reduce their dependence on external powers for defence equipment and technologies. This leads to significant changes in their diplomatic alliances and dependencies.

One of the primary outcomes of localisation is the increased autonomy of the GCC states in their foreign policy decisions. Developing their indigenous defence capabilities makes these countries less susceptible to external pressures and interests. This newfound autonomy enables them to assert their national interests more assertively and independently, thereby shaping regional and international diplomatic relations dynamics. It allows Gulf states to pursue more nuanced and tailored approaches to their foreign policy based on their own security needs and priorities.

Additionally, the localisation process opens up opportunities for establishing new diplomatic alliances and collaborations. As GCC states invest in building their own defence industries, they become attractive partners for other nations seeking to enhance their defence capabilities or expand their influence in the region. This leads to the diversification of the diplomatic network for Gulf states, allowing them to forge new partnerships beyond their traditional allies. By expanding their range of diplomatic relations, the GCC states can navigate regional security challenges more effectively, leveraging different perspectives and resources to achieve their objectives.

However, managing existing alliances and dependencies while transitioning to localised defence industries poses certain challenges. Traditional defence partners, who have been the leading suppliers of equipment and technologies, may view the localisation of defence industries as potential competition. This perception of competition can strain relationships and require careful diplomacy to ensure the transition does not adversely affect longstanding partnerships. Sustaining cooperation with established allies while advancing localised defence industries requires tactful engagement and periodic reassurances. It calls for maintaining open lines of communication and providing reassurances of continued collaboration and opportunities for partnership in new areas.

Moreover, the localisation of the defence industry in the Gulf region has significant geopolitical implications. As the GCC states reduce their dependencies on external powers, it can lead to shifts in power dynamics and influence within the region. Some nations that previously held sway or played larger roles in the Gulf region may seek to realign their partnerships to maintain their influence. This recalibration of alliances can create tensions and opportunities for collaboration among regional and international actors. Gulf states must carefully navigate such shifts, weighing their own national interests against the changing geopolitical dynamics, and proactively engage with partners to ensure a smooth transition.

Another noteworthy outcome of localised defence industries is the potential for greater regional cooperation. As Gulf states develop their defence capabilities, they find common ground in areas of mutual security interests and challenges. This can foster a sense of shared responsibility and the necessity for collaboration on regional security issues. Localised defence industries also enable Gulf states to participate more actively in regional security architectures and initiatives, contributing to collective efforts to enhance stability and address common threats.

Beyond defence-related collaborations, the localisation of the defence industry also opens avenues for diversifying partnerships across various sectors. With the development of technological capabilities and expertise in defence innovation, GCC states can extend their collaborations to sectors such as technology transfer, trade, and infrastructure development. This diversification of partnerships contributes to the overall stability and development of the Gulf region and enhances its integration into the global economy. Increased collaboration in areas beyond defence strengthens economic ties and promotes knowledge-sharing, ultimately benefiting all parties involved.

Additionally, the localisation of the defence industry has significant implications for human capital development and skills transfer. As GCC states invest in developing their defence industries, they prioritise fostering local talent and expertise, which in turn drives innovation and economic growth. By nurturing a skilled workforce, GCC states can attract foreign investment and talent, further enhancing their capabilities in defence and other sectors. This focus on human capital development opens doors for broader collaborations in research and development, knowledge exchange, and capacity building.

Furthermore, localised defence industries contribute to technological advancements within the region. The GCC states stimulate innovation and technological progress by investing in research and development. This promotes self-sufficiency and reduces technology dependence on external suppliers, strengthening national security. In addition, developing advanced defence technologies can create opportunities for collaboration and knowledge-sharing with other nations at the forefront of defence innovation, fostering an exchange of ideas and expertise.

In conclusion, localising the defence industry in the GCC states has profound implications for diplomatic alliances and dependencies. It facilitates increased autonomy in foreign policy decision-making, provides the potential for establishing new alliances and collaborations, presents challenges in managing existing partnerships, induces geopolitical shifts, fosters greater regional cooperation, and drives diversification of partnerships across sectors. Striking a balance between sustaining longstanding alliances and forging new ones will be crucial as the GCC states redefine their diplomatic relations in the era of localised defence industries. Moreover, the localisation process offers opportunities for human capital development, technological advancements, and broad-based collaborations that drive economic growth and contribute to the overall stability of the Gulf region.

Chapter 33

Geopolitical Implications on Regional and International Relations

*A*s the Gulf Cooperation Council (GCC) states embark on localising *their defence industries, significant geopolitical implications exist for both the region and international relations. The development and growth of local defence industries can reshape power dynamics in the area and beyond, influencing alliances, dependencies, and cooperation.*

At a regional level, the localisation of the defence industry has the potential to reduce vulnerabilities and enhance resilience among the GCC states. By minimising external dependencies on arms imports, these countries can develop their indigenous capabilities, leading to a shift in their security posture. This independence in defence production allows for a greater ability to respond to regional threats and contingencies while reducing reliance on external powers and avoiding potential political and economic influence from foreign suppliers.

Localised defence industries also provide economic benefits to the region. Establishing defence manufacturing facilities creates job opportunities for local populations, stimulates technological advancements, and encourages knowledge transfer. This, in turn, helps diversify the economies of the GCC states by promoting high-tech industries and reducing their dependence on hydrocarbons. The economic stimulus generated by defence industries further strengthens the geopolitical standing of the GCC states, boosting their influence in regional and international affairs.

The localisation of defence industries also has implications for recalibrating regional alliances. As GCC states strengthen their indigenous capabilities, their relationships with traditional defence partners such as the United States and European countries may be reevaluated. While these alliances are unlikely to be completely dissolved, there may be a shift in the balance of power, where the GCC states become more self-reliant and assertive in regional security affairs. This shift could lead to new forms of cooperation and partnerships between GCC states and potential collaborations with other emerging powers.

Moreover, the localisation of defence industries enables the GCC states to have greater control over their military technologies and strategic decision-making processes. They can tailor their defence capabilities to specific regional challenges, adopting cutting-edge technologies and strategies that align with their unique geopolitical and security interests. This enhanced autonomy in defence production strengthens the sovereignty of GCC states and fosters a sense of national identity and pride.

On an international level, the localisation of defence industries in the GCC states can significantly impact global geopolitics and geo-economics. As these countries develop their local defence industries, they become potential competitors in the global defence market. This can disrupt the traditional dominance of major defence exporters like the United States, Russia, and China. The rise of local defence industries in the GCC states may introduce new players and increase competition, potentially reconfiguring global defence trade patterns and influence.

Furthermore, localising defence industries in the GCC states can contribute to regional stability by reducing the risk of arms races and potential conflicts. Historically, reliance on foreign suppliers for defence equipment and services has created imbalances, fuelling tensions among neighbouring states. However, with localised defence industries, the GCC states can establish a more level playing field, mitigating insecurities and promoting a cooperative security environment. This can encourage regional dialogue, cooperation, and confidence-building measures, thereby reducing the escalation risk and enhancing the region's peace and stability.

Additionally, the localisation of defence industries in the GCC states has regional and international security implications. Integrating advanced technologies, such as artificial intelligence (AI) and autonomous systems, into indigenous defence capabilities introduces new dimensions in warfare and security. These technologies can enhance the GCC states' ability to address emerging threats, particularly in cyber warfare, hybrid warfare, and maritime security. Developing and deploying advanced defence systems within the region may also have implications for stability and deterrence, potentially influencing regional power dynamics and the balance of power with neighbouring states.

Regarding diplomatic relations and collaborations, localising defence industries in the GCC states may require rediscovering alliances and dependencies. As these countries become more self-sufficient in defence production, their relationships with external defence partners may be impacted. This shift could lead to changes in diplomatic alignments and the formation of new alliances or strengthened regional cooperation mechanisms. The localised defence industry can potentially catalyse greater cooperation in defence research and development, joint exercises, and interoperability among regional partners.

In the context of regional rivalries, the localisation of defence industries raises interesting questions about the competition between the GCC states. While developing indigenous defence capabilities is intended to enhance each country's self-reliance and security, it could also lead to increased competition for limited resources and markets. The emergence of multiple defence industries in the region raises the question of how these states will coordinate and cooperate to avoid duplicating efforts and maintain efficient resource allocation. Balancing the pursuit of independent capabilities with collective security interests becomes crucial to avoid undermining regional cohesion.

Moreover, localising defence industries in the GCC states requires careful consideration of intellectual property rights and technology transfers. As these countries invest in developing their indigenous defence capabilities, they may seek foreign partnerships and collaborations to fill technological gaps or acquire specialised knowledge. However, negotiations around technology transfers could become complex, as the GCC states aim to protect their intellectual property and maintain control over critical defence technologies. Balancing the exchange of knowledge and technology with national security interests becomes an essential diplomatic and strategic challenge.

Furthermore, the localisation of defence industries in the GCC states can have broader implications for the balance of power in the Middle East and the global energy market. As countries in the region reduce their reliance on hydrocarbons and diversify their economies, the geopolitical dynamics surrounding energy resources may be reshaped. The combination of localised defence industries and economic diversification initiatives can enhance the resilience and stability of the GCC states, reducing their vulnerability to fluctuations in oil prices and potential disruptions in the global energy market. This, in turn, could potentially influence their position and influence in regional and international affairs.

In conclusion, the localisation of defence industries in the GCC states holds significant geopolitical implications for regional and international relations. This ongoing process can reshape power dynamics, recalibrate alliances, disrupt global defence trade patterns, strengthen regional security, foster new forms of cooperation and collaboration, and influence broader facets such as regional rivalries, intellectual property rights, and the global energy market. As the GCC states continue to invest in developing their indigenous defence industries, these implications will undoubtedly continue to evolve, requiring careful analysis and strategic considerations from policymakers and defence officials. The positive economic, technological, and security impacts of the localised defence industry in the GCC states make it a transformative development with far-reaching consequences for the region and beyond.

Chapter 34

Potential for Greater Regional Cooperation

*I*n recent years, the Gulf Cooperation Council (GCC) states have recognised the immense potential for greater regional cooperation in the defence industry, leading to a renewed focus on collaboration and joint efforts in research, development, production, and export. The push for localisation and indigenisation of the defence sector has driven member states to explore the benefits and opportunities of working together.

Research and development are key areas where greater regional cooperation holds immense potential. By pooling resources, expertise, and knowledge, GCC states can tackle complex technological challenges more effectively. Collaborative R&D initiatives can yield faster innovation, cost-sharing, and the creation of cutting-edge defence technologies that address the region's specific needs. Joint research projects, for example, could focus on developing advanced cybersecurity systems to protect critical infrastructures or enhancing intelligence-gathering capabilities through artificial intelligence in surveillance and reconnaissance operations. By sharing information and leveraging each other's strengths, GCC states can improve their innovation capacity and stay competitive in a rapidly evolving global defence landscape.

Furthermore, sharing capabilities and knowledge in defence production can enable GCC states to enhance their self-reliance and reduce dependencies on external suppliers. Currently, most of the defence equipment and systems in the Gulf region are imported, making it vulnerable to disruptions in the global supply chain and potential political tensions. Establishing joint ventures, developing reciprocal technology transfer programmes, and creating regional defence industrial clusters can lead to increased efficiency, economies of scale, and the emergence of a competitive and sustainable defence industry. Through joint production efforts, GCC states can manufacture essential defence equipment locally, such as armoured vehicles, military aircraft, and naval vessels, ensuring a continuous and reliable supply. This bolsters the region's defence capabilities and stimulates the member states' economic growth and job creation.

Another area where regional cooperation can offer significant benefits is in defence training and capacity building. The Gulf region faces many security challenges, including terrorism and maritime security threats. By coordinating efforts and resources, GCC states can establish joint military exercises, training programmes, and educational institutions, cultivating a strong and skilled defence workforce. This would enhance the capabilities of individual member states and promote interoperability and cohesion among the armed forces. By conducting joint training exercises, GCC states can develop standardised procedures, improve command and control structures, and foster a shared understanding of operational tactics. Additionally, collaborative efforts can extend to specialised training institutions in counterterrorism, intelligence analysis, and cybersecurity, providing a well-rounded and highly proficient defence workforce capable of addressing diverse security threats.

In addition to the direct advantages, greater regional cooperation in the defence industry can have profound ripple effects on wider economic and diplomatic relations among GCC states. Collaborative defence projects can foster trust, deepen political ties, and strengthen regional security. This, in turn, can pave the way for enhanced economic integration, trade, and investment opportunities. As the GCC states present themselves as a unified market for defence-related products and services, they can attract foreign investment and become a hub for the defence industry. This would boost economic diversification efforts and lead to knowledge transfer, technology diffusion, and developing high-value industries in the region. By leveraging their defence cooperation, member states can project a united front and enhance their diplomatic influence on the global stage, positively impacting regional stability and security.

However, several key challenges must be addressed to realise the potential for greater regional cooperation fully. Firstly, political sensitivities and historical rivalries among member states could hinder the progress of collaborative efforts. GCC states must prioritise collective security and set aside conflicts for the greater good of regional cooperation. This can be achieved through diplomatic dialogue, confidence-building measures, and the development of shared strategic goals. Secondly, varying levels of technological capabilities among member states can pose challenges. To overcome this, knowledge-sharing programmes, capacity-building initiatives, and technology transfer agreements need to be established to bridge the gap and enhance the overall competence of the region. This can be facilitated through targeted investments in research institutions, fostering collaboration between academia and industry, and providing financial incentives to attract and retain skilled professionals.

Furthermore, establishing a clear framework and mechanism for collaboration is crucial for ensuring the smooth flow of information, resources, and expertise. Regular high-level meetings, joint committees, and formal agreements can provide structure and governance to facilitate effective cooperation. Additionally, fostering a culture of transparency and trust among member states is essential to overcoming potential barriers and building a solid foundation for enduring partnerships. This can be achieved by creating joint operating procedures, information-sharing platforms, and dispute-resolution mechanisms. By nurturing an environment of mutual respect and understanding, the GCC states can establish a successful regional defence cooperation model that can inspire other regions facing similar security challenges.

In conclusion, the potential for greater regional cooperation in the defence industry among GCC states is vast. The member states can achieve strategic autonomy, develop cutting-edge technologies, and strengthen their defence capabilities through collaboration in research and development, defence production, training, and capacity building. Moreover, regional cooperation can contribute to wider economic integration, diplomatic relations, and stability in the Gulf region. It is imperative for the GCC states to capitalise on this potential and work collectively towards a more united and self-reliant defence industry. By doing so, they can position themselves as key players in the global defence landscape, safeguard their interests, and contribute to regional security and prosperity.

Chapter 35

Conclusion

This book has comprehensively examined the evolution and implications of GCC states' localisation of their defence industries. Throughout the chapters, we have delved into the historical background of the defence industry in the GCC states, the role of arms imports in shaping military capabilities, and the driving factors behind the push for indigenisation and self-reliance. Moreover, we have explored the economic implications, security considerations, and geopolitical ramifications associated with this strategic transformation.

The GCC states have long relied on arms imports to meet their defence needs. This heavy reliance on external suppliers has resulted in concerns over the vulnerability of military capabilities in times of political discord or international disputes. The desire for greater autonomy and self-sufficiency in defence capabilities has thus propelled the localisation of defence industries in the GCC states.

The localised defence industry efforts in the GCC have yielded notable economic implications. By developing local defence industries, these states aim to diversify their economies, reduce dependence on a single sector, and foster technologically advanced industries with high value-added potential. With an increasing focus on research and development in conjunction with defence production, the GCC states seek to cultivate indigenous innovation and technological expertise. This, in turn, opens up avenues for knowledge transfer, job creation, and the growth of associated sectors such as aerospace engineering, software development, and advanced manufacturing.

Moreover, by localising their defence industries, the GCC states stand to benefit from improved security considerations. The ability to domestically produce military hardware, including weapons systems, munitions, and advanced technologies, enhances their self-reliance and reduces vulnerabilities associated with international tensions or disruptions in supply chains. Furthermore, indigenisation efforts allow for greater control over the maintenance, repair, and upgrades of defence systems, ensuring operability and readiness even during political or economic strain.

The localisation of defence industries also carries significant geopolitical implications. It represents a shift in the balance of power and influence within the Gulf region and globally. As the GCC states aim to reduce their reliance on external powers for defence capabilities, it challenges established patterns of global defence trade. It fosters a rearrangement of relationships and dependencies. This can potentially lead to the emergence of new centres of technological prowess and influence worldwide.

From a security standpoint, the localisation of defence industries presents opportunities for integrating advanced technologies. These advancements, such as artificial intelligence, cyber security, robotics, and unmanned systems, can augment the defensive capabilities of the GCC armed forces. With a localised defence industry, the GCC states can adapt and adopt cutting-edge technologies to address emerging threats in areas such as hybrid warfare, cyber-attacks, and unmanned aerial systems. This bolsters their defence capabilities and positions them at the forefront of regional security cooperation and innovation.

Diplomatically, the localisation of defence industries fosters the potential for greater regional partnerships and collaborations. The GCC states can establish themselves as reliable and capable contributors to regional security by cultivating indigenous defence capabilities. This has the dual benefit of enhancing their diplomatic standing and promoting regional stability. Through strengthened defence ties with like-minded countries, the GCC states can simultaneously advance their own security interests and contribute to broader security cooperation mechanisms in the region.

In conclusion, localising defence industries in the GCC states represents a transformative endeavour with multidimensional implications. Prioritising the development of indigenous defence capabilities strengthens national security, drives economic diversification, and reshapes regional and global power dynamics. To achieve sustainable success, it is crucial for the GCC states to continue investing in research and development, technology transfer programmes, and the nurturing of local talents and expertise. Strategic partnerships and collaborations, combined with ongoing monitoring of geopolitical developments and emerging technologies, will ensure that the localisation efforts remain adaptive and aligned with evolving defence strategies and doctrines.

Chapter 36

Key Findings and Insights

The localisation of the defence industry in the Gulf Cooperation Council (GCC) states has been driven by strategic considerations and the desire for greater autonomy in defence capabilities. These states, including Saudi Arabia, the United Arab Emirates, Qatar, Kuwait, Bahrain, and Oman, have recognised the importance of localising their defence industries to reduce their reliance on foreign suppliers and enhance their self-reliance in times of crisis.

One of the key factors driving the localisation efforts is the desire to minimise external dependencies, particularly in procuring critical defence equipment and technologies. These states have historically relied heavily on arms imports to meet their defence needs, with the United States being the leading supplier. While arms imports have provided a quick and convenient way to acquire advanced military equipment, they have also posed challenges regarding long-term sustainability, technology transfer, and potential vulnerabilities associated with dependency on foreign suppliers.

The GCC states have significantly developed their indigenous defence industries to address these concerns. This localisation process involves various stages, including establishing domestic defence firms, joint ventures with international defence companies, technology transfers, and investment in research and development. These efforts aim to enhance their defence capabilities, create skilled job opportunities, foster technological innovation, and contribute to economic growth.

Some successful examples of defence industry localisation can be found in Israel and Turkey. Israel has developed a robust defence industry, with companies such as Israel Aerospace Industries (IAI), Rafael Advanced Defence Systems, and Elbit Systems becoming global players in defence technology. This localisation has created jobs and economic growth, allowing Israel to maintain technological superiority and strategic autonomy.

Similarly, Turkey has invested significantly in its defence industry over the past few decades. With companies like Roketsan, ASELSAN, and Turkish Aerospace Industries (TAI), Turkey has been able to produce its own tanks, helicopters, unmanned aerial vehicles, and missiles, thus reducing its dependency on imports. The success of Turkey's defence industry localisation has positioned it as a regional power and a major defence exporter.

The localisation of the defence industry in the GCC states carries economic implications beyond job creation and innovation. It can diversify their economies and reduce their reliance on oil revenues. By establishing defence industrial bases, these states can attract foreign investments, promote technology transfer, and develop high-tech manufacturing capabilities that can be applied in other sectors.

Furthermore, localisation efforts aim to enhance the resilience and readiness of the GCC states' armed forces. By reducing dependency on foreign suppliers, these countries can ensure the timely availability of critical defence equipment and technologies during times of crisis or embargo. This self-reliance is particularly crucial in a region that faces various security challenges, including regional conflicts, terrorism, and asymmetric threats.

The localisation of the defence industry in the GCC states also has significant geopolitical ramifications. It can influence power dynamics within the region and beyond, potentially shifting the balance of power and reshaping global geopolitics and geo-economics. As these states develop their indigenous defence industries and become less reliant on traditional defence suppliers, it may lead to a redistribution of influence and alliances. The growing influence of local defence industries could also impact global defence trade, with potential implications for the defence industries of other countries.

In addition to the economic and geopolitical dimensions, the localisation of the defence industry has important security implications. By integrating advanced technologies, such as artificial intelligence, autonomous systems, and cyber capabilities, the GCC states can enhance their defence capabilities and strategies in areas such as cybersecurity, hybrid warfare, and maritime security. These technologies can provide a competitive edge and better protect critical infrastructure and national interests.

The localisation of the defence industry necessitates reevaluating diplomatic relationships and collaborations. As the GCC states develop their indigenous defence industries, they may seek to redefine their alliances and dependencies. This could lead to regional and international relations shifts and potentially foster greater regional cooperation and integration. Countries with established defence industries, such as the United States, Europe, and Russia, may need to adapt to these changes and find new avenues for collaboration.

Furthermore, the localisation of the defence industry can have social and technological benefits. The GCC states can nurture a culture of innovation and scientific discovery beyond defence applications by investing in research and development. These advancements can spill over into other sectors, such as healthcare, telecommunications, transportation, and energy, contributing to societal progress and economic diversification.

The localisation of the defence industry also presents opportunities for collaboration and knowledge-sharing among GCC states. These countries can accelerate their defence industrialisation efforts and establish a strong regional defence ecosystem by pooling resources, expertise, and technologies. This collaboration can enhance their respective capabilities and foster a sense of collective security and mutual trust.

However, some challenges associated with defence industry localisation need to be addressed. Developing advanced defence technologies often requires extensive research, development, and testing, which can be time-consuming and expensive. Additionally, building a skilled workforce and fostering a culture of innovation requires long-term education, training, and infrastructure investments.

Moreover, defence industry localisation may face resistance from established defence suppliers who may perceive it as threatening their market share and strategic interests. This resistance can manifest in various forms, including lobbying efforts, export controls, and restrictions on technology transfer. Overcoming these challenges requires effective policies, strong leadership, and international cooperation.

In conclusion, the localisation of the defence industry in the GCC states has far-reaching implications for their security, economy, diplomacy, and regional dynamics. It is a complex and multifaceted process that requires careful consideration and coordination. Policymakers and defence officials should take note of the key findings and insights presented in this chapter to inform strategic decision-making and future prospects in the defence sector. Further research is warranted to delve deeper into specific aspects of the localisation process and its holistic impacts.

Chapter 37

Recommendations for Policy Makers and Defence Officials

.1 Foster Collaboration and Cooperation

One of the key strategies for policymakers and defence officials is to actively promote collaboration and cooperation among the Gulf Cooperation Council (GCC) states. The benefits of a localised defence industry can be maximised through joint research and development projects, sharing of expertise, and coordinated procurement strategies. The Gulf nations can pool their resources and expertise by working together, achieving economies of scale and enhancing their collective security.

Establishing collaborative frameworks such as joint military exercises, intelligence sharing, and joint training programmes can build trust and interoperability among the GCC states. It can offer an opportunity for defence officials to exchange best practices, enhance operational capabilities, and strengthen the effectiveness of the region's defence forces as a whole. Additionally, establishing joint defence research and development centres can facilitate knowledge sharing, synergy, and the joint development of cutting-edge defence technologies.

4.2 Develop Comprehensive National Defence Plans

Each GCC state should develop comprehensive national defence plans that align with their goals for the localisation of the defence industry. These plans should outline objectives, strategies, and timelines for achieving self-reliance in key defence capabilities. By clearly defining the path towards self-sufficiency, policymakers and defence officials can facilitate the allocation of resources, monitor progress, and ensure adherence to strategic goals.

These plans should prioritise investment in research and development, technology transfer, and human capital development. Robust research and development programmes will enable the GCC states to create indigenous defence technologies, reducing reliance on foreign suppliers. Partnerships with international defence companies can facilitate technology transfer and provide opportunities for local defence industries to acquire advanced capabilities and expand their expertise.

To nurture a skilled workforce effectively, establishing specialised defence training institutes and academies can provide tailored education and skills development programmes. These institutions would focus on defence engineering, cybersecurity, artificial intelligence, and other emerging technologies. Also, fostering partnerships with universities and research institutions can create a collaborative ecosystem, encouraging knowledge exchange and promoting cutting-edge research in defence-related fields.

4.3 Enhance Education and Skills Development

Investing in education and skills development is essential for successfully developing a localised defence industry. Policymakers should prioritise the establishment of specialised defence universities and vocational training centres that provide comprehensive education in defence-related fields. These institutions should offer degree programmes, professional certifications, and hands-on training opportunities to cultivate a pool of skilled professionals capable of driving innovation and effectively operating and maintaining locally produced defence equipment.

Scholarship programmes and research grants can be introduced to attract top talent to the defence industry and encourage the development of a highly skilled workforce. Policymakers can ensure a sustainable pipeline of skilled professionals to support the defence sector's growth by offering financial incentives and educational opportunities to those interested in pursuing careers in defence technology and engineering.

Furthermore, collaboration between the defence industry and academia should be fostered to enable knowledge transfer and collaborative research. Strategic partnerships with universities and research institutes can provide defence companies access cutting-edge research, state-of-the-art facilities, and specialised expertise. This collaboration will not only enrich the academic environment but also enhance the capabilities of the local defence industry through applied research.

4.4 Promote Technology Transfer and Partnerships

Seeking partnerships and technology transfer agreements with international defence firms can accelerate the development of local defence capabilities. Policymakers and officials should actively engage with renowned defence suppliers, particularly those with advanced defence industries, to establish relationships promoting technology transfer, knowledge sharing, and joint development projects.

These partnerships must be structured to ensure the transfer of critical technologies in a manner that safeguards national security interests, promotes indigenous research and development, and allows the GCC states to develop their own indigenous capabilities in the long run. Establishing technology transfer policies and agreements that balance the need for local innovation and self-reliance with access to advanced defence technologies will be crucial.

Moreover, fostering partnerships with international defence companies can provide access to global supply chains, creating opportunities for local defence industries to participate in international defence programmes and benefit from economies of scale. These partnerships can also facilitate the transfer of manufacturing know-how and quality control processes, enabling the local defence industry to meet international standards and compete in global markets.

4.5 Establish Regulatory Frameworks and Incentives

Policymakers should establish clear and favourable regulatory frameworks to encourage investment in the defence sector. These frameworks should balance stimulating growth and ensuring international standards and norms compliance. By creating an enabling environment for local defence companies, policymakers can attract private sector investment and promote the establishment and growth of a robust defence ecosystem.

In addition to favourable regulations, incentives such as tax breaks, grants, and subsidies can be offered to local defence companies. These incentives should stimulate research and development activities, promote innovation, and attract domestic and foreign direct investments. By reducing financial barriers and offering support to defence startups and small and medium-sized enterprises (SMEs), policymakers can create an entrepreneurial ecosystem conducive to the growth of the defence industry.

Policy makers should establish mechanisms for effective oversight and control alongside regulatory frameworks and incentives. Robust governance and compliance mechanisms will ensure that the defence industry adheres to ethical practises, safeguards national security interests, and operates in alignment with international non-proliferation commitments.

4.6 Prioritise Research and Development

Investment in research and development is crucial for the long-term success of the localised defence industry. Policymakers and defence officials should allocate adequate funds and resources to support research and development initiatives focusing on cutting-edge technologies and innovation. This investment will facilitate the development of advanced defence capabilities, enable the GCC states to stay at the forefront of defence technology and address emerging security challenges.

Furthermore, establishing defence research and development centres dedicated to specific technology areas, such as cybersecurity, unmanned systems, advanced weapon systems, and space technologies, can provide a platform for collaboration among academia, defence industries, and government entities. These centres can drive research efforts, support technology incubation, and foster innovation in critical defence domains.

Policy makers can introduce funding mechanisms such as grants and incentives for defence-focused research projects to encourage research and development activities. These mechanisms would attract researchers, innovators, and entrepreneurs to the defence sector, creating a culture of innovation and technological advancement.

4.7 Build Strategic Partnerships with Academia and Research Institutes

Collaboration between the defence industry and academia fosters innovation and drives research and development. Policymakers should actively encourage and facilitate strategic partnerships between defence companies and universities/research institutes. Such partnerships can facilitate knowledge transfer, collaborative research projects, and joint technology development.

Establishing industry-led research centres within academic institutions can promote close collaboration between defence companies and researchers. This co-location of expertise would allow academia and industry to collaborate on cutting-edge research, address complex defence challenges, and translate research outcomes into practical solutions. Such partnerships can also provide valuable opportunities for students and researchers to engage in applied research and gain industry exposure, helping to bridge the gap between academic knowledge and practical application.

Furthermore, mechanisms such as joint appointments, sabbaticals, and industry-sponsored research projects can facilitate the exchange of ideas and expertise between academia and the defence industry. By supporting these collaborations, policymakers can bridge the gap between theoretical research and practical application, contributing to the growth of the defence industry's innovation ecosystem.

4.8 Maintain a Balance between Localisation and International Cooperation

While localisation of the defence industry is desirable, policymakers and defence officials must also recognise the importance of international cooperation and collaboration. The defence industry operates in a globalised world, and international partnerships and alliances are essential for addressing common security challenges, promoting interoperability, and accessing advanced defence technologies.

Policymakers need to strike a balance between localisation efforts and international cooperation. Localisation should not be pursued at the expense of cutting off ties with international defence suppliers and partners. Instead, policymakers should aim to develop a defence industry capable of meeting domestic security needs while maintaining strong relationships with international partners.

International cooperation can offer several benefits to the localised defence industry. It can provide access to advanced technologies, expertise, and global supply chains, thereby enhancing the capabilities and competitiveness of the local defence sector. Collaboration with international defence companies can also facilitate knowledge transfer, innovation, and exposure to best practices in the global defence industry.

Moreover, international cooperation can contribute to regional stability and security. The GCC states can strengthen their collective security and deter potential threats by engaging in joint military exercises, intelligence sharing, and coordinated defence efforts. Partnerships with other like-minded nations can also promote a rules-based international order and contribute to global peace and security.

Therefore, while prioritising localisation efforts, policymakers and defence officials should ensure that the defence industry remains globally connected and open to collaboration. This can be achieved through establishing strategic partnerships, participation in international defence programmes, and adherence to international standards and regulations.

4.9 Strengthen Defence Export Capabilities

To sustain the growth and development of the localised defence industry, policymakers and defence officials should prioritise expanding defence export capabilities. Building a robust defence export sector can generate revenue and economic growth and enhance the GCC states' profile and reputation as credible defence suppliers.

Policymakers should invest in market research and analysis to identify potential export opportunities and target markets. Market intelligence can help prioritise investments, allocate resources, and tailor defence products and services to meet the specific needs of target customers. A deep understanding of customer requirements and market dynamics is essential for successful defence exports.

In addition, policymakers should establish a clear regulatory framework for defence exports that ensures compliance with international laws and norms. Export control regulations and licencing procedures should be in place to prevent the proliferation of sensitive defence technologies and safeguard national security interests. Adherence to international non-proliferation commitments is vital to maintaining the reputation and credibility of the GCC states as responsible defence exporters.

Furthermore, policymakers can support defence companies through export promotion programmes, trade missions, and financial incentives. These initiatives can help defence exporters access new markets, build relationships with potential customers, and navigate the complexities of international defence trade. Support can also be extended through diplomatic channels, with policymakers actively engaging with foreign governments to facilitate defence export deals and strengthen bilateral defence relationships.

4.10 Monitor and Evaluate Progress

Continuous monitoring and evaluation of progress is essential to ensure that policies and strategies effectively achieve the goals of localisation and self-reliance in the defence industry. Policymakers and defence officials should establish key performance indicators (KPIs) and benchmarks to measure progress, identify gaps, and make informed decisions.

Regular reporting and review mechanisms should be implemented to track the implementation of national defence plans, monitor resource allocation, and assess the impact of policies and initiatives. These mechanisms will provide policymakers and defence officials with valuable insights into the effectiveness of their strategies and enable them to make necessary adjustments and refinements.

In addition, policymakers should foster a culture of accountability within the defence industry. Establishing mechanisms for independent audits and evaluations can ensure transparency, identify inefficiencies, and promote best practices. Clear accountability frameworks will create a culture of continuous improvement and enable stakeholders to learn from successes and failures.

Furthermore, policymakers should engage in regular dialogue with industry stakeholders, academia, and research institutions to solicit feedback and gather insights on the progress of localisation efforts. This engagement will help identify challenges and bottlenecks, address industry concerns, and ensure that policies and strategies remain relevant and aligned with the evolving needs of the defence sector.

By actively monitoring and evaluating progress, policymakers and defence officials can make informed decisions and steer the localisation efforts toward maximising the benefits for national security, economic growth, and technological advancement.

Chapter 38

Future Prospects and Areas for Further Research

T he localisation of the defence industry in the Gulf Cooperation Council (GCC) states holds significant promise for regional self-sufficiency, technological advancement, and economic diversification. As the GCC states continue to invest in developing their defence capabilities, exploring the prospects and identifying key areas that require further research is imperative. This chapter delves deeper into these prospects and outlines the research areas contributing to comprehensive understanding and effective decision-making.

1. Technological Advancements:

The future of the defence industry in the GCC states lies in embracing technological advancements. Further research is required to assess the transformative potential of emerging technologies such as artificial intelligence (AI), unmanned systems, and autonomous technologies. Understanding the implications of these technologies in defence operations, including autonomous platforms, intelligent surveillance systems, and

AI-driven decision-making, will shape the strategic focus and investments in the defence industry localisation efforts.

Research in this area should also explore the integration of advanced sensors, data analytics, and cybersecurity technologies into the defence sector. Robust theoretical and experimental frameworks can aid in designing and implementing cutting-edge solutions to address evolving security challenges.

Moreover, research endeavours should focus on understanding the ethical, legal, and societal implications of emerging technologies in defence, including autonomy, privacy, and accountability issues. Establishing guidelines and frameworks that govern these technologies' responsible adoption and usage will be crucial for maintaining public trust and international standards.

2. Defence Exports and Global Markets:

Expanding the defence industry's presence in global markets is critical to future prospects. Further research is needed to identify potential market demands, assess competition dynamics, and evaluate the feasibility of defence exports. Comprehensive market analysis should consider regional and international security dynamics, evolving defence procurement trends, and opportunities for collaboration with partners and allies.

In-depth research is required to identify the defence products and capabilities that GCC states can offer to global markets. This analysis should assess exportable technologies, including missile systems, unmanned aerial vehicles (UAVs), advanced communication systems, and cyber-defence tools. Understanding market requirements, regulatory frameworks, and export restrictions in different regions will aid in developing tailored strategies for entry into global defence markets.

3. Collaborative Research and Development:

Fostering collaborative research and development (R&D) efforts is pivotal to the future growth of the GCC defence industry. Research in this area should focus on identifying potential areas for collaboration, establishing dedicated R&D centres and institutions, and facilitating knowledge sharing among GCC states and other countries with advanced defence industries. These collaborative efforts can lead to technological advancements, cost-effective solutions, and sharing best practices.

The research should also explore joint projects and partnerships with leading global defence industry players and research institutions. Establishing research networks and consortiums focusing on shared areas of interest, such as cybersecurity, digital defence technologies, and advanced materials, will facilitate knowledge exchange and accelerate progress.

Furthermore, studying successful models of defence-industry cooperation, such as the European Defence Agency (EDA) and NATO's Smart Defence initiative, will provide insights into how GCC states can foster regional cooperation for R&D, resource-sharing, and joint defence capabilities development.

4. Exportable Technologies and Intellectual Property Rights:

Protecting innovation, intellectual property, and exportable technologies is crucial for the prospects of the GCC defence industry. Further research is needed to assess existing intellectual property rights regulations, identify gaps, and develop comprehensive frameworks that safeguard locally developed technologies.

Research should also focus on fostering a culture of innovation within the defence industry, encouraging research and development, and incentivising intellectual property creation. Establishing technology transfer agreements, licencing frameworks, and export control mechanisms will ensure the proper utilisation, monetisation, and protection of intellectual property in the defence sector.

Additionally, research should explore the potential for developing and marketing exportable technologies unique to the region. This can involve utilising the GCC states' geopolitical advantages, climatic conditions, expertise in desert operations, maritime defence, and critical infrastructure protection.

5. Cybersecurity and Information Warfare:

With the evolving threats posed by cyberattacks and information warfare, further research is needed to develop local capabilities. Understanding the region-specific challenges and vulnerabilities and assessing current cybersecurity initiatives will aid in formulating effective defence strategies.

Research efforts should focus on analysing the threat landscape in cyberspace and conducting vulnerability assessments to identify potential risks and mitigation strategies. Exploring opportunities for regional collaboration in cybersecurity research, training, intelligence sharing, and joint exercises will enhance the collective resilience of the GCC states.

Furthermore, research should address the human element of cybersecurity and information warfare, including awareness programmes, capacity building, and professional development to ensure a skilled and knowledgeable workforce capable of defending against emerging threats.

6. Environmental Sustainability and Green Defence Initiatives:

The prospects of the GCC defence industry should align with global sustainability goals. Further research is needed to assess the feasibility and potential benefits of incorporating green defence initiatives. This research should explore renewable energy integration into military operations, resource efficiency, environmentally friendly manufacturing practices, and waste reduction.

Developing sustainable defence practices will reduce the industry's ecological footprint and promote environmental stewardship. Research should assess the potential for renewable energy adoption in military bases, facilitating the development of energy-efficient platforms and systems and exploring the use of bio-based materials in defence manufacturing.

Furthermore, investigating the economic benefits and opportunities associated with green defence initiatives, such as job creation in clean technology industries, will provide a comprehensive understanding of the potential social and economic impact.

7. Future Warfare Scenarios:

Anticipating and preparing for future warfare scenarios is critical for the GCC states' defence industry. Research should assess emerging trends, technologies, and threats to develop robust defence strategies and capabilities.

Further research is required to analyse and understand hybrid warfare scenarios, which combine conventional, irregular, and cyber warfare tactics. This research should focus on assessing the impact of hybrid warfare on defence systems, doctrine, and capabilities development.

Additionally, research should explore asymmetric threats posed by non-state actors, terrorist organisations, and cybercriminals. Understanding the potential risks and vulnerabilities associated with these threats will aid in designing effective countermeasures, intelligence gathering, and response mechanisms.

Furthermore, emerging technologies such as hypersonic weapons, directed energy systems, and quantum technologies will undoubtedly shape the future battlefield. Research should analyse their potential applications, implications, and countermeasures to ensure the GCC states remain at the forefront of defence technology.

8. Socio-Economic Impact Assessment:

Understanding the socio-economic impact of defence industry localisation is vital for holistic planning. In-depth research is needed to evaluate defence industry growth's direct and indirect effects on job creation, skills development, and economic diversification efforts.

Assessing the potential spillover effects of defence expenditures, evaluating the multiplier effect of defence industry investments on other sectors, and examining the long-term sustainability of defence-related jobs will provide policymakers with valuable insights for promoting a balanced and resilient economy.

Furthermore, research should explore the potential risks and challenges associated with over-reliance on the defence sector, including the vulnerability of a defence-centric economy to global fluctuations and the need for diversification into non-defence industries.

Conclusion:

The prospects of localisation of the GCC defence industry are multi-dimensional and hold great potential for regional security and economic prosperity. Extensive research in technological advancements, defence exports, collaborative R&D, intellectual property rights, cybersecurity, environmental sustainability and green defence initiatives, future warfare scenarios, and socio-economic impact assessment will contribute to comprehensive understanding, effective decision-making, and successful implementation.

By exploring the transformative potential of emerging technologies, such as AI, unmanned systems, and autonomous technologies, further research will help GCC states leverage these advancements to enhance defence capabilities, improve decision-making processes, and address evolving security challenges. Understanding these technologies' ethical, legal, and societal implications will also be essential for responsible and accountable adoption.

Research in the area of defence exports and global markets will enable GCC states to identify potential market demands, assess competition dynamics, and develop tailored strategies for entry into global defence markets. Understanding market requirements, regulatory frameworks, and export restrictions will be crucial for successful export initiatives.

Fostering collaborative R&D efforts is pivotal to the growth of the GCC defence industry. Research should focus on identifying potential areas for collaboration, establishing dedicated R&D centres, and facilitating knowledge sharing among GCC states and other advanced defence industry players. Learning from successful models of defence-industry cooperation will provide valuable insights for regional collaboration.

Protecting innovation, intellectual property, and exportable technologies is critical for the prospects of the GCC defence industry. Further research is needed to assess existing intellectual property rights regulations, develop comprehensive frameworks, and foster a culture of innovation within the defence industry.

With the evolving threats of cyberattacks and information warfare, further research is needed to develop local cybersecurity and information warfare capabilities. Understanding region-specific challenges, conducting vulnerability assessments, and exploring opportunities for regional collaboration will enhance the collective resilience of the GCC states.

Integrating environmental sustainability into the defence industry is crucial. Further research should explore the feasibility and benefits of incorporating green defence initiatives, such as renewable energy integration, resource efficiency, and environmentally friendly manufacturing practices. Investigating the economic benefits and opportunities associated with green defence initiatives will provide a comprehensive understanding of their potential impact.

Anticipating and preparing for future warfare scenarios will be critical for the GCC defence industry. Research should assess emerging trends, technologies, and threats to develop robust defence strategies and capabilities. Analysing hybrid warfare scenarios, asymmetric threats, and emerging technologies will ensure the GCC states stay at the forefront of defence technology.

Assessing the socio-economic impact of defence industry localisation is essential for holistic planning. Research should evaluate the direct and indirect effects on job creation, skills development, and economic diversification. Understanding the potential risks and challenges associated with over-reliance on the defence sector will inform policymaking for a resilient and balanced economy.

In conclusion, the prospects of the GCC defence industry localisation are vast and require extensive research in various areas. By embracing technological advancements, exploring global markets, fostering collaborative R&D, protecting intellectual property, addressing cybersecurity challenges, embracing environmental sustainability, preparing for future warfare scenarios, and assessing socio-economic impacts, the GCC states can achieve self-sufficiency, technological advancement, and economic diversification in the defence industry.

References For Further Reading

Bibliography

Abdulla, Abdulkhaleq."The Gulf Security Architecture: Partnership with West Asia" Palgrave Macmillan Publishers Limited, 2014, London.

Algosaibi, G.A. (1993). Gulf Crisis (1st ed.). Routledge.

Al-Tamimi, Mohammed Mousa Kadhim & Paul Schulte (eds.), "GCC Military Cooperation Towards Joint Arab Action", Abu Dhabi Strategic Debate Papers Series- Vol 8., Emirates Centre for Strategic Studies and Research (ECSSR), 2017, UAE.

Anicetti, J. (2024). Defence Offsets and the Global Arms Trade: Explaining Cross-National Variations (1st ed.). Routledge.

Ball, N., & Leitenberg, M. (Eds.). (1983). The Structure of the Defense Industry: An International Survey (1st ed.). Routledge.

Cordesman, A.H. (1984). The Gulf And The Search For Strategic Stability: Saudi Arabia, The Military Balance In The Gulf, And Trends In The Arab-Israeli Military Balance (1st ed.). Routledge.

Cordesman, Anthony H. "Arms and Oil: U.S. Military Strategy and the Persian Gulf", HarperCollins Publishers, 1987, New York.

Fattah, Zainab & Donna Abu-Nasr, "Saudi Arabian Defence Market:

Spending Forecast to 2029", ASD Media BV Publishing,2020, Amsterdam.

Haglund, D.G. (Ed.). (1989). The Defence Industrial Base and the West (1st ed.). Routledge.

Hartley, K., & Belin, J. (Eds.). (2019). The Economics of the Global Defence Industry (1st ed.). Routledge.

Heradstveit, D. (2004). Oil in the Gulf: Obstacles to Democracy and Development (H. Hveem, Ed.) (1st ed.). Routledge.

Hill, Fiona et al., "Gulf Security in the Twenty-First Century", Diane Publishing Co., 1997, Pennsylvania

Katz, D.H. (2020). Defence Diplomacy: Strategic Engagement and Interstate Conflict (1st ed.). Routledge.

Knights, Michael. "The Military Balance in a Shattered Levant: Conventional Forces, Asymmetric Warfare & the Struggle for Syria", The Washington Institute for Near East Policy Publications, 2013, USA.

Koleilat Khatib, D., & Maziad, M. (Eds.). (2018). The Arab Gulf States and the West: Perceptions and Realities – Opportunities and Perils (1st ed.). Routledge.

Louth, J. (2023). Understanding UK Defence Exports: The International Trade in Defence Capabilities (1st ed.). Routledge.

Lutterbeck, Derek. "Small States and Alliances", Springer Publishing, 2001, New York.

Markowski, S., Hall, P., & Wylie, R. (Eds.). (2009). Defence Procurement and Industry Policy: A small country perspective (1st ed.). Routledge.

Pridham, B.R. (Ed.). (1985). The Arab Gulf and the West (1st ed.). Routledge.

The International Institute for Strategic Studies (IISS), (Ed.). (2020). ISR and the Gulf: An Assessment (1st ed.). Routledge.

'Arafāt'Alā' al-Dīn. *Regional and International Powers in the Gulf Security*. Cham: Palgrave Macmillan, 2020.

Almezaini, Khalid S, and Jean-Marc Rickli. *The Small Gulf States*. Taylor & Francis, 2016.

Alterman, Jon B, and Kathleen H Hicks. *Federated Defense in the Mid-*

dle East. Rowman & Littlefield, 2015.

Ashraf Mishrif, Yousuf Al Balushi, and Springerlink (Online Service. *Economic Diversification in the Gulf Region, Volume II : Comparing Global Challenges*. Singapore: Springer Singapore, 2018.

Baabood, Abdulla. "Dynamics and Determinants of the GCC States' Foreign Policy, with Special Reference to the EU." *The Review of International Affairs* 3, no. 2 (December 2003): 254–82. https://doi.org/10.108 0/1475355032000240702.

Bajusz, William D. *Arms Sales and the U.S. Economy*. Routledge, 2019.

Barany, Zoltan. *The Political Economy of Gulf Defense Establishments*. Cambridge University Press, 2021.

Çağlar Kurç, Richard A Bitzinger, and Stephanie G Neuman. *Defence Industries in the 21st Century*. Routledge, 2021.

Cordesman, Anthony H. *Bahrain, Oman, Qatar, and the Uae*. Westview Press, 1997.

———. *National Security in Saudi Arabia*. Bloomsbury Publishing USA, 2005.

———. *Saudi Arabia*. Routledge, 2019.

———. *The Gulf and the West*. Routledge, 2019.

Cordesman, Anthony H. *Bahrain, Oman, Qatar, and the Uae : Challenges of Security*. Boulder: Taylor and Francis, 2018.

Deger, Saadet. "Economic Development and Defense Expenditure." *Economic Development and Cultural Change* 35, no. 1 (October 1986): 179–96. https://doi.org/10.1086/451577.

DesRoches, David , and Dania Thafer. *The Arms Trade, Military Services and the Security Market in the Gulf States*. Gerlach Press, 2016.

Edwin Daniel Jacob, and Springerlink (Online Service. *Rethinking Security in the Twenty-First Century : A Reader*. New York: Palgrave Macmillan Us, 2017.

Efraim Inbar, and Benzion Zilberfarb. *The Politics and Economics of Defence Industries*. Routledge, 2013.

Gaub, Florence. *An Arab NATO in the Making?* Createspace Independent Publishing Platform, 2016.

Hossein Askari, Amin Mohseni, and Shahrzad Daneshvar. *The Milita-*

rization of the Persian Gulf. Edward Elgar Publishing, 2009.

Kaddorah, Emad Y. *The Rise of the GCC States and Turkey*. Cambridge Scholars Publishing, 2021.

Khalid Al-Jaber, and Dania Thafer. *The Dilemma of Security and Defense in the Gulf Region*. ISD LLC, 2019.

Martini, Jeffrey, Becca Wasser, Dalia Dassa Kaye, Daniel Egel, and Cordaye Ogletree. *The Outlook for Arab Gulf Cooperation*. Rand Corporation, 2016.

Nadkarni, Vidya. *Strategic Partnerships in Asia*. Routledge, 2010.

Saab, Bilal Y, and Atlantic Council Of The United States. *The Gulf Rising: Defense Industrialization in Saudi Arabia and the UAE*. Washington, Dc: Atlantic Council, 2014.

Şaban Kardaş, and Bülent Aras. *Geopolitics of the New Middle East*. Taylor & Francis, 2023.

Sadellah, Abir. "The Defence Industrial and Technological Base of the Gulf Countries :: Observatoire of Arab-Muslim World and Sahel :: Foundation for Strategic Research :: FRS." frstrategie.org, April 18, 2019. https://frstrategie.org/en/programs/observatoire-du-monde-arabo-musulman-et-du-sahel/defence-industrial-and-technological-base-gulf-countries-2019.

Sim, Li-Chen, and Jonathan Fulton. *Asian Perceptions of Gulf Security*. Taylor & Francis, 2022.

Tan, Andrew T H. *Research Handbook on the Arms Trade*. Cheltenham, Uk ; Northampton, Ma, Usa Edward Elgar Publishing, 2020.

Thafer, Dania. *Creative Insecurity*. Hurst Publishers, 2023.

Tsouras, Peter G. *The Greenhill Dictionary of Military Quotations*. Greenhill Books, 2020.

Warren, D.H. (2021). Rivals in the Gulf: Yusuf al-Qaradawi, Abdullah Bin Bayyah, and the Qatar-UAE Contest Over the Arab Spring and the Gulf Crisis (1st ed.). Routledge.

Yazīd Şāyigh. *Arab Military Industry*. Potomac Books, 1992.

Data From Open Sources:

[1] https://www.sipri.org/sites/default/files/2023-03/2303_at_fact_s
heet_2022_v2.pdf

[2] https://www.sipri.org/sites/default/files/2022-03/fs_2203_at_20
21.pdf

[3] https://www.sipri.org/publications/2023/sipri-fact-sheets/trends
-international-arms-transfers-2022

[4] https://www.csis.org/analysis/changing-trends-gulf-military-and-s
ecurity-forces-net-assessment

[5] https://www.sipri.org/databases/armstransfers

[6] https://www.sipri.org/sites/default/files/2021-03/fs_2103_at_20
20.pdf

[7] https://www.sipri.org/sites/default/files/files/FS/SIPRIFS1010.p
df

[8] https://www.sipri.org/publications/2022/sipri-fact-sheets/trends
-international-arms-transfers-2021

[9] https://www.sipri.org/media/press-release/2022/global-arms-trad
e-falls-slightly-imports-europe-east-asia-and-oceania-rise

[10] https://www.sipri.org/sites/default/files/2019-05/fs_1905_gulf
_milex_and_arms_transfers.pdf

[11] https://www.aljazeera.com/news/2021/3/15/global-arms-transfe
rs-level-off-but-middle-east-imports-grow